The Courage to Own my Truth

From Hidden Pain to Healing Light

Elisabeth G Henderson

Table Of Contents

Dedication

This book is dedicated to performing artists and arts administrators who have suffered in silence from sexual and political abuse by their teachers and colleagues.

You have worked hard for most of your lives to perfect your craft out of a deep love for the beauty and emotion of your art form. You have changed my life in ways I could have never imagined possible. Playing music, attending concerts, and attending performances have all made me completely different. I admire you all for what you do, and I can't thank you enough for the joy and healing your performances have brought into my life.

I admire your strength, tenacity, and commitment to creating beautiful experiences for people like myself who didn't have the chance to commit their whole lives to performing arts. Now that I spend all my social and free time at concerts, musicals, and operas, attending performances fills me with much hope and wonder.

It never gets old. Whether I know you were there, I've seen you in America or abroad. I admire your work and pray your passion endures. Regardless of what you've been through, how others have treated you, or how you thought of yourself, I want to let you know I believe you are important, and your actions hold significance. You all have my heart.

This book is for the professional artists, administrators, and organizers who have landed their dream careers in the world's top organizations and those who have landed their dream careers in their country or city's organizations who dedicate their lives to enriching the world with their gifts.

I also dedicate this book to performing artists who have felt their gifts and talents are insignificant and will never receive the attention, validation, help, or support they deserve. Your gifts matter in a world where power abuses and fear prevail.

If you haven't auditioned yet, if you're a perfectionist with stage fright, or if you're afraid of auditions, you matter. Your gifts and talents matter too.

This book offers guidance for those who desire to provide themselves with what they've lacked. If you have lost your confidence or sense of self, you matter, and your desires matter.

Thank you to all artists striving for excellence despite being used and abused. Please keep blessing and healing the world with their gifts every day. We appreciate and love you. All of you who dance, sing, play, or act have a place in this world, in my heart, forever.

Acknowledgments

Writing this book has been among the most exciting and enlightening experiences ever. None of this would have been possible without the love and encouragement of my first life coach, Jean Dorff, who taught me to accept and love myself after the sexual assault I experienced. The publishing of his book and my assault happened in the same year. God knew I would need it. I am forever grateful to him for encouraging me to write a book about my experience.

Dina-Marie Weineck, thank you for showing me how to love myself without judgment, persist in challenging times, and build a thriving business that supports me and the inspiring clients I help and serve every week. Thank you for putting courage back on the menu in my life.

My dear older sister Ruthie, we have been through so much together. Thank you for leading by example, always encouraging, and showing me what it is to believe in oneself.

The Courage to Own My Own Truth

Thank you, Uncle Steve, my wildly successful, creative, and favorite uncle, for always being there to talk and guide me through my career and life transitions.

Thank you to Corrina da Fonesca Wolheim for reminding me I am a writer whose stories and thoughts need to be heard. Your creativity and ability to innovate how music listens inspire me and others worldwide.

Anastasia Boudanoque, you have such a big heart. Thank you for taking me under your wing. Your wisdom and support have been invaluable to me in my career.

Kristy Odom, thank you for leading by example and always being willing to lend an ear

Lawrence Jordan, thank you for educating me on the mystical side of the universe. You have opened my eyes to see other worlds.

Pastor Melinda Blaze, I had stopped believing in much of anything before I met you. Thank you for practicing what you preach and teaching me to do the same. Your wisdom, compassion, love, and support remind me of how good God always is.

Chris Klement, thank you for your sound advice and support. Thank you for showing our community that a little boy from the trailer parks of El Paso could positively affect a vast community. Your commitment to making my community a better place is truly inspiring.

Dr. Andrew Gill, thank you for everything and for sharing your wisdom and understanding with me for many years. I would not be alive without your support.

Edith Majors, your gift of perception and foresight has enabled me and many others to understand myself and tap into my intuition like never before.

Also, thank you to my teachers here at home who believe in me, my abilities, and this story. My life could not have changed for the better without you.

Background

My parents were born and raised in the sticks of South Carolina in the mid-20th century. They were both among the first people in their families to complete their four-year college education. They faced all kinds of atrocities while trying to complete their education but are very proud of the resilience and hard work they put into making it to the middle class. I grew up in the suburbs with my parents and older sister.

When we first moved to Texas, my dad immediately lost his job, and my parents were often at odds and under stress.

Alcoholism-related violence has claimed many lives on both sides of my family. In our home, we could not express anger or emotion that made my mother uncomfortable. However, she could express any emotion she felt at any time. I didn't know it, but my mom suffered from a severe mental illness on top of being abused by extended family members throughout her life. My father is a quiet but friendly man who bottled his anger and let it all out a few times per year.

The Courage to Own My Own Truth

As children, my sister and I would often unsuccessfully try to break up fights between each other. At times, police would come to our home to resolve their conflicts, and we lived in constant fear of a fatal outcome. Being seen as weak and lame for not ignoring violence, my parents would scream at me for being upset about them fighting, berating me for being upset, and trying to stop the fights.

I hated the feeling of helplessness inside when I didn't know what was going to happen next, and wanting to be anywhere but home was the perfect cocktail for a pattern of avoidance of my scary feelings. Freeze response became my regular response to any distress.

At some point, when there was chaos in our home, I would hide, fighting the urge to intervene; being so frightened, I would have to run to the bathroom to combat diarrhea. To self-soothe, until the age of 9, I would wet the bed, suck my thumb, and shred my navel with sharp objects until I was into adulthood. My parents would yell at me in sheer terror when I would bleed from my navel, wanting even to know why I had skin-picking habits and why I would not stop.

Many black Americans lack family skills due to neglect and abandonment. Part of it is personal, and part of it is based on age. Among African Americans in the USA, there is an obsession with identifying with royalty. I believe that this obsession comes from the fact that 70% of Black American children do not have a father in their lives. I have people in my family who try to identify with royalty, hoping to understand their importance and feeling like they have a purpose.

Despite not knowing their father, they still claim titles like King and Queen and seek to cope with abandonment, unaware that actions speak louder than any label or title. Some of us have experienced emotional and physical neglect and abandonment in every way. Still, emotional neglect has had a potent impact on the way I perceive myself and others. My parents got some things very right, and some things they got very wrong, just like all emotionally immature parents do. From the time I was young, I felt like my needs were a burden to my caretakers, and this feeling stayed with me.

Before the incident of sexual abuse, I was a person who despised emotions I deemed uncomfortable. The feeling of having needs was the worst feeling I could think of, next to the feeling of expressing them. During my upbringing, I was conditioned to believe that authorities knew best and my decision-making was flawed.

No one urged me to pursue my truth, preventing me from being honest with myself. Growing up, my only understanding was always to give my best performance, regardless of how I felt. Acknowledging feelings of fear and stress, I was told I was not trusting God enough. I constantly shut down certain parts within me, not even realizing their existence, because of the intense resistance I had towards certain emotions.

Before my sister and I were old enough to attend school, my mom taught us the alphabet, numbers, colors, and prayers. She constantly told us that the more books we read, the more powerful and knowledgeable we would be. Since my mom was a librarian, I watched videos and read books in the library while she worked.

The Courage to Own My Own Truth

I loved watching ballet and musical performances and would often imagine that I was dancing on a stage. Usually, I would beg my parents to send me to dance classes, but they never did. They told me it was too expensive and I needed to focus on my core studies. Despite performing well in my core studies, I always had my heart and mind set on creative pursuits that I knew I wouldn't receive support for.

When I started school, my teachers were concerned about my constant daydreaming and refusal to speak or take part in class. As a child, I daydreamed about being an adult and being free to do anything. My teachers often notified my parents of my absent-mindedness in class, and they were usually accurate. I was in another world; I was in a world with Warren Beatty, often fantasizing that Dick Tracy would come to pick me up from school and we would make a wonderful life together.

My thoughts and other worlds consumed me often as the people in my surroundings failed to recognize or support my desires. The following year , my teacher brought my parents in for a conference and told them I seemed to be here in body only, but my mind always seemed elsewhere.

She mentioned calling my name or asking me questions and that I would just be staring off, seeming to be in another world. They were unaware that I was in another world. I was in a world where I could express myself entirely without shame. Since I did not feel empowered enough to express myself in the outside world, I would create worlds where I could meet that need. Every year at school, the teachers would organize story-writing competitions for each grade. As an avid reader, I would be so excited to write stories about girls who would find answers to their questions by being brave and free.

When my mom discovered I was daydreaming in class, she took me aside and told me she didn't understand why. It looked awful and made her and my father look bad, and I had to stop and get myself together, or I would have to repeat another grade. I wouldn't say I enjoyed being incompetent or not enough again. Having already felt that way before when I was in kindergarten, I promised myself to get my act together no matter how I felt. I focused and achieved without embarrassing myself or my family.

The Courage to Own My Own Truth

I was at the top of my class the following year in every subject. I was expected to maintain straight As in all subjects, and I usually did. As a child, I strongly desired knowledge and enjoyed teasing classmates who didn't read or learn as much as I did. I loved winning spelling Bees, writing contests, and art and poetry recitation competitions held by my school. I love the positive attention I received for speaking in front of a group and creating stories and art that others didn't feel free enough to start. Able to stand getting second place, I tried to ensure it rarely happened. In high school, I wanted to take performing arts outside of school, but my parents said no. Deep down inside, I always felt like my natural gifts were being ignored to some extent. I knew deep down inside that my parents were not recognizing my authentic self and that I could do more with my artistic gifts than I could do. During high school, I continued to participate in dance, it was the only thing that made me feel alive and the reason I wanted to go to school. By the time I got to college, I had chosen a generic major with which I could do many things. To avoid being perceived as incompetent again for selecting a useless degree, I pursued a degree that would provide flexibility in various fields so I wouldn't be limited to one specific area.

I didn't realize then that choosing such a generic major would eventually make me feel dead inside because my innate gifts and talents were not being used as they were. I became very depressed and down in the dumps during my third year in undergrad college when I realized what I had done what I've been doing. It felt late to change my major to performing arts, a path I should have pursued since childhood to make a living. When I started seeing a psychologist about the depression that I was going through, they suggested I take antidepressants, exercise more, and get fresh air. Retaking medication was not the route I wanted to go. I would feel better doing something creative and artistic outside of my studies. After I left the doctor's office, I set out to manage my depression, but it had to do with artistic expression. I knew I would not make a living in anything creative. Deciding to give a voice to that part of me, I felt better, but didn't know how to begin. Overwhelmed by thoughts of survival, I struggled to decide what I "should" do.

One week after I saw the doctor, I went to a Wellness Fair and found a natural way to ease my emotional distress. When I arrived at the Wellness fair, many things were going on.

Three people hula hooping, practicing Tai chi drumming, and a drumming circle. I had no clue where to start. But then I noticed a sound. I could feel it as much as possible, sounding resonant and beautiful. I didn't know what to do with that myself. It made me wonder where that sound was coming from. I turned, looked to my right, and saw an older man playing the harp in his lap. The harp was relatively small, but the sound was huge. He asked why I was here, and as I searched, I explained I sought a natural cure for depression. He seemed surprised, and he asked me if I had ever tried sound therapy; I said no, thinking to myself it sounded ridiculous and probably like something that wouldn't work, but I'd instead try sound therapy rather than another drug.

When the man handed me the harp, I picked it up, sat on the grass, and started playing. I thought to myself, the sound is reverberating beautifully through my body. This feels like true love. There's a way like vibrating, you know, whole body girl, sounding so angelic. I continued playing as he left to catch up with his friends. A little while later, I saw him approaching me. I looked around, and I saw everyone packing up to leave.

I asked him where everybody was going, and he told me I had been sitting there for almost two hours.

I started playing the harp, and I was astonished. I couldn't believe it, so he asked me if I would like to rent a harp home and invited me to his and his wife's home to pick a harp, so that weekend I went to their house and chose a harp to rent. When I arrived at his home, a fortress of harps greeted me. I had never seen so many harps in my entire life. His ex-wife greeted me warmly and asked if I wanted to learn to play with a teacher. I told her I didn't intend to learn, being too old, but still wanted to rent a harp. That day, I left with the names of people in my area with harps for sale and looked at a few.

My harp and I became inseparable. When I was away from my harp, all I could think about was its sound and the music I could play. It was like the harp was causing me to remember parts of me I had lost when I was a child. I felt compelled to do something with the music inside me. For the first time in many months, I felt so alive. I finally had something I could call my own and looked forward to being alone with me and my instrument.

From Hidden Pain to Healing Light

While driving, working, and going about my day, I daydreamed of playing music. It didn't matter to me; I didn't know the notes or the technique.

Could I express myself through sound like the older man said? He shared that he had fought cancer for years and found joy and healing in the sound of the harp. When he first said this, I thought yeah, right, but as I spent more time with my heart, I felt the same way he felt, even though I didn't want to admit it then. When I connected with others who felt the same way I did, I could accept that an instrument could bring me so much hope and be something to look forward to daily. In time, I had no problem romanticizing playing it, playing the harp how I wanted to because I knew other people out there felt the same way. I'll tell some professional musicians about this feeling; some will look at me funny, and others will relate with me completely.

Unsure that if my parents had allowed me to pursue performing arts as a job, I would have felt as passionate about it as I do now. I think it's because playing music isn't my job that I see it this way. Had I chosen music as a profession, my emotions might have been different.

Now, I think God had me come across music again as an adult to bring me hope and trust in myself and Him.

As a young adult, learning to play music, learn different dances, and watch myself improve from week to month, month to month, and year to year helped me establish trust in myself. For example, I would choose a song to learn and bring it to my teacher. Let's work on it together in a lesson, and then I'll continue improving this song daily, week after week, and month after month. The same thing went for dance. Learning different dances helped me establish trust in myself and my ability to learn and create something beautiful and emotionally fulfilling simultaneously. Playing music felt both addictive and intoxicating to me. Transferring the ability to commit to improving my artistic hobbies to my academic career helped me develop trust in myself to improve my grades, relationships, and quality of life. Progressing in life brought beautiful and rewarding experiences. Even today, when I sit down to play my instrument, I can get frustrated, but I remind myself that as this piece improves, other areas of my life improve similarly. I can acknowledge them with love and even enhance them through fear, frustration, and doubt.

Part I: The Abuse

The Incident of Abuse

I was in grad school, finishing my last semester the month before I experienced a sexual assault. I was very stressed about a particular class I was taking, and I couldn't get my mind off of the class. My father had fallen sick and was in the hospital. I could not eat at all. I was so stressed about the class and my father's health, wondering if he'd be able to make it to my graduation and if he was going to be okay, feeling paralyzed with fear. All I could think about was my father and his health, wondering how things were going to turn out for him and me. My mind began conjuring images of complete disaster. I felt so paralyzed and worried about the future as I thought about the worst thing that could and might happen to my father. All I could think was that everything was going wrong when I needed it to go right, and I could do nothing to stop it.

Fortunately, with the support of my classmates and colleagues, I scored "A" in the class, and my father's health improved, and he made it to my graduation in good health. I was so relieved and happy that everything worked out. Feeling like I could eat and breathe again, I became more involved in my local social clubs, hobbies, and associations and was excited about my future.

The following semester, I read through a harp magazine featuring a well-known prodigy harpist. He had played in 40 countries worldwide and was coming to my city to perform and give harp lessons. He was handsome and talented, and people worldwide raved about his performances. I immediately called my teacher and told her I wanted to see him perform. She informed me that the harp society in my city would host his visit and that he would be in my town for two weeks. I was so excited that I had never seen a man play the harp, much less a handsome man. Six months later, when he arrived in our city, we were excited about taking his classes and attending his performance. His performance was incredible.

After he performed, my teacher introduced me to him, and instantly, I felt like he was looking through me. He asked if I was coming to his birthday dinner with the board after the concert, and I said yes. During the reception, we talked, and he barely paid attention to the students trying to speak to him. He focused wholly on our conversation and paid little attention to anything else. The last thing I thought about was that he genuinely found me attractive.

I thought he was a bit of a flirt, but I was sure he probably had a lot of girlfriends all over the planet because he's super handsome and fun to talk to.

As I walked around the venue and spoke with other students and teachers, they talked about how funny, intelligent, handsome, and attractive he was. Some talked about how wonderful it was to take private masterclasses with him, and He seemed to understand what problems they were facing and how to handle those problems. I wasn't his student, but I wanted to know more about his creative process.

Later that evening at the restaurant, he sat at the head of the table, making all of us laugh with his dark, dry sense of humor. I sat a few seats away from him next to my teacher. He and I kept making eye contact. Somehow, I felt like I was the center of his attention, and we weren't even talking to each other. When it was time to leave, a board member asked me to drop him off at his hotel on my way home, and I told her I could take him. As we stood to leave the restaurant, he came behind me, put his hand on my lower back, and asked me if I was driving him back to where he was staying. I told him yes. We got in my car and talked about his concerts, teaching, the beautiful places he had visited worldwide, and his plans to visit other states and countries during the year.

When we arrived at the house, I felt nervous as we talked. He seemed here, but not here. The next day, Macie had to go out of town and asked me to drop him off for her at his hotel so he could catch his plane the next day. I agreed to drop him off after I got off work.

While I was at work the next day, he texted me constantly. That day, I had a major deadline to meet, and I worried I would be late picking him up. I was very late, but he did not seem to mind. He asked me if I wanted to have dinner before I dropped him off at the hotel. I agreed and took him to my favorite Tex-Mex restaurant.

At dinner, we had a great conversation. He was so hilarious and listened closely to everything I said. I told him about the pieces I was learning, and he advised me on how to approach the music and encouraged me to stop judging myself so harshly. He joked I seemed to be the type of person who judges the air breathed. We laughed a lot. He seemed to listen and understand my lack of patience, encouraging me to enjoy the learning process and not be so harsh with myself. After discussing my insecurities, music theory, etc., I felt better about improvising.

After dinner, I drove him to the hotel. He had five bags, so I helped him take his bags inside his room. As I turned to leave, he kissed me. Not surprised, I told him I had to leave. He restrained me with his arms and pushed me onto the bed.

The Courage to Own My Own Truth

As I struggled, I asked him if he was going to rape me. His eyes turned completely black, and he screamed, "I could rape you!". I stopped struggling and looked to my left and saw myself watching us as he pushed me onto the bed. The other me said, "Don't struggle, Elisabeth. He likes this."

Suddenly, the other me disappeared, and I felt like I was back in my body. I thought, "Why did you come in here, Elisabeth?" You saw how he looked at you. How could you be so stupid? He let me go. As I sat up, bolted out of the room, and ran as fast as I could, I could not feel my legs; I could feel my heart pounding in my ears, and I was out of breath. I stopped at the end of the hall to catch my breath and turned around. He stood in the hall, staring at me. He wasn't moving.

I ran out of my car, jumped in, and locked the door. I started laughing with my heart still pounding in my veins and thought, "You nearly got raped. That was a close call." Relief swept over me as I laughed to myself. That was a close call, I thought. You are so lucky that you fought and ran; that could have been so bad. What I didn't realize was how bad it was going to get.

A few weeks later, I could not sleep. My abuser sent me a text message at 3 am saying, "Hey, what's up?" I was furious. Where the hell are you? It's 3 am. I asked him.

Why were you getting aggressive and crazy when I tried to help you move your things into your room? He seemed confused. "I wasn't getting aggressive with you. I could tell you liked it, though." I must have re-read that text message 100 times. He cannot be serious, I thought. Why would he text me after I ran from them out of pure terror? I told him he was utterly terrible. He told me he wasn't being aggressive, just anxious, and didn't mean to terrify me. "Well, you did," I told him. As I sat in the dark with my mind racing, I seriously thought about telling the people who had arranged his visit what he did to me. All I could think of was that he had spent time with other young women teaching, and I wondered if he had done something similar to them.

Since he had young teenage students, I asked if he had abused them or tried anything crazy with them.

It made my skin crawl to think that he could be a serial rapist living right under the nose of my community. I hoped and prayed that he would never come back, utterly amazed that he had no remorse for his violent, disgusting actions. My mind spun as I could not shake the feeling of being watched. This feeling would not go away for a long time.

Abuse of Power

What happened to me was just after the Me-Too movement had hit in 2017. All I could think of was the fact that I'd heard these horror stories about people being abused by people in power. I couldn't understand why the authorities hadn't caught and imprisoned the individuals responsible for these acts. But now I knew why people didn't tell. The situation was just so dark, sick, and awful and something that you don't want your name associated with. I couldn't understand how people were getting away with it, but now I had in my mind that I know these women in Hollywood and other industries don't tell because it's too shocking.

What happened to me was unbelievable, and then I could not get it out of my head. I wondered who would believe me. Wanting to tell someone in power and wondering who else he was trying to victimize, I felt like I would risk sounding crazy. How was I going to prove what he did to me? I kept the text messages he sent me in case I needed to use them as evidence in case I needed them if I ever had the balls to tell on him.

It wasn't until later, when I met other women and men who are in the classical music and performing arts industries who told me their horror stories, that I realized that this was an actual thing that happens all the time and that people were afraid to talk about it because they were afraid what could happen to their careers just like the women in Hollywood and many other industries and organizations. What's going to happen? I knew this person would attack me by teaching children and adults, and I wondered what he had done to them.

It was only a year later, when his teachers were in prison for sexual abuse, that I realized that this was something that some people tried to pass on to their victims.

Some victims will stay silent, while other victims will create more victims. I was so insulted that he had treated me like this. Who did he think he was? Why couldn't he be a sane person? What had happened to him to make him believe that this was OK? Why do I feel so burdened by this?

Proclamations of the Support of Women

This incident occurred right before I started working as an organizer and volunteer in the classical performing arts industry.

I felt confused and shocked at what these people could get away with. I asked why these men were not being treated like criminals after they did something so sick and evil. Still, I felt sorry for the women who kept what was happening to themselves for so long, but I wondered if they told someone what these men were doing to them.

Many people knew what was happening but feared what would happen if they spoke up. Even though I did not understand how complicated it was, I knew that the people in power were taking advantage of men and women.

I didn't realize that those in power could get away with what they had been doing for decades, which just blew my mind. I figured at some point, someone was going to go crazy and kill their abusers for ruining their lives, careers, and mental health.

Today, when people think of rapists and sexual abusers, most people think of hardened criminals on the news with 50-page wrap sheets. Most people do not think of the people around them as predators. Still, predators are usually famous people looked up to, highly educated, and well-liked, and who get away with violating and intimidating people for so long. I came to understand that people were afraid of these abusers and what they could do to them, and that was the reason they told no one.

I can think of many times I've seen in the news being a teacher of the year, coach of the year, or a pastor or caregiver who is well-liked by and popular with many people who have turned out to be sexual predators. In the classical performing arts scene, the predators are typically people of influence, conductors, directors, and teachers who prey on the trust of the people they are supposed to support and serve.

I started volunteering in the arts because of my pure love for music and my appreciation for the artists who worked so hard to produce the music that was so healing. What I did not know, though, is that a lot of the people who I looked up to as artists and those who created programs and pieces of music that I loved so much had been victims of sexual abuse.

But as I worked at different festivals and conferences organizing events for classical performing arts, I saw that there were many people with many stories about very prominent, known, and well-established people in power from a variety of organizations who have abused their power and taken advantage of those subordinate to them. It didn't surprise me when it happened, but people's responses astonished me. The behavior they encountered disgusted some; others made excuses for the behavior or tried to insinuate that the victims were just "sluts" who asked for it. Other people, and we're not able to put into words what had happened to them because they were so traumatized by the abuse and did not even know it.

They knew something was seriously wrong with what the person in power was doing to them. Still, they did not know what to do about it because it's such an awkward and precarious situation to have someone who's supposed to be teaching you or supporting you trying to manipulate you sexually.

Many individuals I came across had spent their formative years alone with their instrument or with people who also played it and had achieved their dream of being a soloist or playing with an orchestra or a chamber group.

Some people I worked with came from conservatories where it was customary to eat, sleep, and play their instrument and nothing else. I deeply respect their single-mindedness, ability to focus on creating beautiful music, and commitment to perfecting their craft. The world of performing arts isn't just about dedication and beauty; it's about perfecting art forms. Many people in this industry have experienced criticism and pressure from a very young age, something that few others have or will ever experience.

Some musicians come from families with enough money to support them until they land their first big job at 30. Many of them also come from families and environments that do not have the resources to give them the education they need to succeed in such a small, elite world. Many people have made considerable sacrifices to send their children to festivals and pay for the teachers they need to get to where they want to go in the field. To reach the top 1% of the orchestra's opera roles and orchestra placements and the coveted dance roles, families must commit lots of time and money for their child to succeed in the field. There is no way around it.

While many beautiful organizations expose poor students to classical music and help children develop an appreciation for and understanding of the art forms, many of those who have achieved their dream in the field come from families who have the resources to help their child succeed in an orchestra, ballet, or opera program that will enable them to reach the top organizations. When people reach these positions, you often see the same people repeatedly from festival to festival worldwide.

Spending just weeks or even summers around high-performing musicians socially was interesting. Some artists I interacted with reminded me of a person who spent time in prison and, after 25 years of solitary confinement, had no clue how to relate to people or understand anything. Some performing musicians know their lives are not relatable to most people; others seem to give it much thought and that people who don't play an instrument for 20 hours per day are strange. The most part of working and socializing with these musicians and opera singers was that many believed they were experts on "social and racial issues" because they played concertos and sonatas for 20 hours daily. Many read news from Instagram and Facebook and have no sense of reality outside of performing arts. Sometimes, I could tell that they were curious about life on the outside, and then other times, they had no clue and were content with not knowing what life outside of Conservatory land was like.

Some of their simplistic explanations for the most complex situations...especially situations they do not understand, are often shocking. They seem to figure their life must be pretty straightforward if someone is not playing an instrument.

Many people who play at an elite level have spent their formative years alone with an instrument and do not know how "normal" people live. They spend all day and night playing their instrument, and the only human interaction they get is social media or spending time with people who live the same type of life.

For people on the autism spectrum, it's even more complex because they don't know how ordinary people do anything. Then, when you hear them trying to explain an incident of sexual abuse, it is too confusing to comprehend.

The elite performing arts is a microscopic world where many teachers in classical performing arts know many people see them as irreplaceable, and therefore, take advantage of as many people as possible because they know students see them as one-of-a-kind and often believe that the only way, they can gain success is if this teacher thinks that they are good enough to get their dream job or dream position that they've always wanted. Many refined their skills of making people feel seen and heard, and they're encouraging and kind towards students so they can gain their trust and take advantage of them.

I have observed that artists are afraid to tell because they fear the backlash they might get from their colleagues, other students, and other people in positions of authority. Their social life, professional life, and personal life are all intertwined in the industry. Some don't even know many people who work outside the industry, so they feel they must protect their reputation or else they could lose everything.

Loyalty vs. Honesty

In the classical performing arts world, there is a war between artists and between loyalty and honesty. Many people are loyal to the art forms and the people who create them because of their deep love for what they do. There is a pervasive inability to separate the person from their work. Some men and women have spent their whole lives holed up in a practice room, missing huge milestones in social development and building social acumen, who commit their lives to working with highly talented teachers. Many of these people feel that if they report abusive behavior to the authorities, then they are letting down the art form and their colleagues who would not believe them.

Many people know that there are many layers of people protecting these abusers from being prosecuted by the law and that if they report to them, then their careers could be over. When people are honest about what has happened to them, others often ignore, blame, or mock them. Those who stand with them often face accusations of opportunism because they were denied something they wanted. This is highly unlikely, considering that they spend 80 percent of their life trying to become "good enough" to work with their abusers.

Recently, I mentioned to someone in classical music how the Julliard School fired a composition teacher named Robert Beaser after over 500 people wrote an open letter online. The letter humiliated the influential teacher and highlighted how he had belittled his students and colleagues throughout his teaching career. I imagine that in the real world if this man was a regular person, he might serve 20 years in state prison for the abuse he subjected his students to. This person said to me, "Well, not all the people who signed the open letter were his students, so that may not be true that he abused people."

These students knew that the only way to get him fired was through an open letter rather than taking the issue to the FBI or law enforcement, which tells me that these students knew their teachers were operating outside the jurisdiction of the law. I often wonder what would happen to them if these people who are too talented go to prison for 25 years. To this day, I find it disgusting that people with a talent in a specific area are above or outside of the law because they have mastered an art form.

Many of the people in charge or at the top of this industry don't see the need to contact law enforcement because they have lived outside of real life for so long. Others don't believe that there is a real problem.

Still, many of the people who are abusing artists in this industry are teaching and living their day-to-day lives at some of the world's most prolific arts institutions.

Often, in social media posts or on these artistic institutions' websites, you'll see proclamations declaring that they stand for diversity, inclusion, and women's rights in the classical arts and so on and so forth.

However, I saw no proclamations that these institutions were ready to fight against the abuse of the performing artists who represented their institutions with the law of the land. My intuition tells me that sexual abuse is one of those filthy and Icky topics that nobody wants to discuss openly because these organizations and institutions know that if they confronted these abusers with the law, many of their teachers and leaders would no longer be working. Addressing the mess they have created and figuring out how to handle it frightens many people. Many people in the performing arts industry may be reluctant to confront the fact that they have been involved in mistreating and manipulating the individuals they claim to help and serve.

The question remains: do the people and authorities who allow these acts of abuse continue to want loyalty, or do they want honesty? Right now, I still believe that people wish for loyalty because they know they live in this tiny, elite, insular world where they made the rules out for everybody else. I think many people want to protect what they've created because if their creation crumbles, it might mean that their world of "perfection" might not be perfect and that they might not be ideal.

Their declarations and proclamations of support may be like a House of Cards about to come down. I'm not sure that many people could handle the fact that what they're supporting, creating, and silenced about for so long is not just imperfect but crude, ugly, illegal, and wrong. When people hold criminals accountable, regardless of their talent, they can uphold the art form to an actual standard of integrity.

The Week After the Incident

In the week after the abuse incident, I was initially quite jumpy. Every sound made me look up suddenly; when I walked to my car, I would look around for signs of danger. On the one hand, I thought telling anybody about this incident was out of the question, and then I thought this person teaches children. I wonder what he does to them. Maybe I should report to him. Oddly enough, it didn't cross my mind to report him to the police. I thought, "I don't want to be associated with this person, shape, or form." What a monstrosity of evil, I thought. I just wanted to forget about the incident altogether. Someone flipping a switch like that and seeming no remorse horrified me.

I wondered who else he was doing these things to and how often he was abusing and terrifying other people. Knowing that he taught children regularly was especially horrifying to me.

Three days after the incident, I went to see my therapist, and I told them about the incident in grave detail.

My therapist became outraged and demanded that I report to the person immediately. You don't understand what I told them. What if nobody believes me or thinks that I'm just being ridiculous? Many people like this person and feel great at what they do. What if people were more loyal to him because he was their teacher? I don't want my name associated with this person, especially in this way. At the pit of my stomach, I had not. My heart kept sinking every time I thought about what had happened. I left my therapist's office that day feeling relieved that I had told someone, but I still wanted to extract this story from my head so I would never have to think about it again. I wanted an apology from this monster, hoping that maybe if he told me he was drunk and psychotic, I could explain away in my mind what happened so I wouldn't have to think about reliving the incident again.

The Courage to Own My Own Truth

A few days later, I sat in a restaurant with a friend having dinner, and I told her everything that had happened. Since I knew she had been a victim of sexual abuse, I thought she would understand. To my relief, she understood completely how I felt. It was such a relief to tell her because I knew she had been through a lot trying to overcome her own traumatic experiences. I told her every single detail of what happened.

She told me that based on my behavior in the past week, I probably had PTSD and that I should report him to the authorities, even though I did not want to. She explained that what happened would hang in my head and overshadow everything until I said something. I dismissed her, stating that I had no desire to be involved with what happened, fearing that the incident could hold me responsible. There was just too much on the line for me to tell anybody. The story was too insane for me to be a part of for the rest of my life. Being so frightened, I couldn't fathom repeating this story to anyone who could do anything about it. I wondered what would happen to me and what would happen to the surrounding people. The whole thing was so embarrassing and disgusting that I wanted to move on. However, that proved to be impossible.

Sometimes, I thought I would see him when I left my home and went grocery shopping, got my nails done, went to the bank, or ran errands. My heart would constantly skip a beat or sink when I looked at people and then realized a few moments later that it wasn't him and he wasn't there. I felt so paranoid that he would come back out of nowhere and attack me. I felt guilty that it had happened, but I couldn't understand where the feelings of guilt were coming from. One part of me kept telling myself you should have seen that coming.... Didn't he seem weird to you? And then another part of me said you got away; you're okay now. Why are you blowing this up in your mind? It's not like someone raped you, and he's nowhere around here. You won't see him again.

Eventually, I sleepwalked. I did not have a history of sleepwalking, but I remember sometimes, in the middle of the night, I would wake up in different parts of my apartment and not know how I had gotten there. Sometimes, I would put away dishes in my bedroom closet without recollection of ever putting them there. Other times, I would sleep on the floor in a distinct part of my apartment, not knowing how I got there when I woke up.

On one hand, I felt like I existed only in my mind, and in another way, I felt like I did not live anywhere.

No matter how desperately I tried to go through the motions, day-to-day things worsened. The days and the nights seemed to blur together as I fell into a haze, feeling like I did not exist anywhere.

The flashbacks- sleepwalking, bedwetting, internet addiction and whiskey

Having horrific dreams about him was just the beginning. Most days, I put it out of my mind by filling my days with my usual activities, concerts, plays, Internet surfing, and spending time with friends. Even though I filled my days with my regular activities, I started seeing him in my dreams because of the suppression of my thoughts. A few times a week, I saw his face staring at me and screaming, daring me to move on. It was like I could feel him thinking about the incident, like he regretted that I had gotten away and that he didn't get what he wanted.

The Courage to Own My Own Truth

I didn't even want to sleep because I didn't want to have dreams about being attacked. After having a few weeks of very little sleep, I requested sleeping pills from my doctor.

After a few weeks, the pills stopped working. Once again, I was upset that I could not sleep and started taking my pills with tequila to help them work better. Then, one night, I passed out on the couch, and my roommate attempted to wake me up, but I remained unresponsive. She told me she was shaking me for 5 minutes and thought that I was dead. I told her I had a bit to drink but was okay. Why was she making it such a big deal? I thought. People sleep hard after consuming all the time, and I just needed my rest. What a drama queen! I wished she would leave me alone.

Around the same time, I started wetting the bed. Having not wet the bed since I was nine, I wondered what was happening to me. I figured I just needed to stop drinking with the sleeping pills, and I would be okay again.

The Courage to Own My Own Truth

One night on the 4th of July weekend, I was scrolling through Facebook, waiting for my friend to come to pick me up from my apartment, and there, the abuser popped up on my feed. He was on the BBC talking to the camera. The camera zoomed in on his eyes exceptionally quickly, and I had the worst panic attack of my life. I could not catch my breath as I fell to the ground, huffing and puffing. I felt so sick and weak on the inside. My head was spinning as I tried to catch my breath. Feeling like I was going to suffocate to death, I lay down on the ground as my body's temperature rose; I sweat; I closed my eyes and passed out.

Later, I woke up to the sound of my phone ringing. My friend called to tell me they had arrived at my apartment to pick me up. I stood up, finished putting on my makeup, and went outside to meet them. Quickly, I stored my panic attack and fainting episode in the back of my mind, scolding myself for freaking out and telling myself that I should stop dwelling on such a negative experience and that I should have the strength and inner resources to move on. This shouldn't be so hard, I thought. Maybe I should research resilience online and get myself some help.

Things are fine. Why can't I get it together?

A few months later, I found a beautiful new residence to move into, got a promotion and raise at work, and even purchased a new car I loved. My new place to live made me feel excited. Feeling like there was so much to be grateful for that year, I told myself that if I could focus on the things that I could be grateful for, then the thoughts of the incident should go away. The upbeat new experiences were exciting, and I was progressing in many areas of life, so how could I still be dwelling on the incident? Still, a sense of heaviness in my body built within me, and I ignored it.

The whole time I was going on with my life, I wondered if he was doing this to other people and why I let him go. Should I be ashamed of letting him off the hook like I did? My resentment towards myself was eating me alive in ways I did not even know. On the one hand, I was constantly telling myself that I was okay because he did not live in my country and did not know where I lived, and another part of me just wanted this feeling to go away. The sense of being in two minds around the incident was something that I hated myself for.

My body continued to feel heavy and tired, and there was no way I was going to face what happened again.

Most of the time, I just told myself I was a talented, cheerful person who needed to get on with her life. How could I be so weak to let a monster like him determine my feelings? Didn't I have the inner resources to pull it together and move on? It's not like he beat me up or something. I wasn't pregnant. Why am I reacting like this? I'll be fine. As I tried to busy myself with new goals and opportunities around my hobbies and interests, I felt stuck, but I did not want to attribute the feeling to what had happened to me. I figured that so many things were happening around me so fast that I needed to adjust to the recent changes, and I would be fine.

The Struggle to Remain Numb

When I started working at my new job, I was relieved that I already knew how to do most of the tasks, and the workload wasn't as heavy. Still, as I worked, I found starting the tasks I was supposed to be doing very difficult. I just chalked it up to the stressors of being in a new environment and tried harder to start tasks, but every task seemed overwhelming, no matter how small.

Why was I feeling so heavy and tired all the time? The job wasn't so difficult. I was in a new building at the organization. Even though I had been in the building for a few months, I was still trying to figure out how to get around the building, but every time I would leave my office and go down a corridor or open a door that I had never opened before, I would find myself completely lost. After several months in this position, I could still not find my way around the building. Sometimes, I would get lost near my office and have to ask employees I didn't know to help me get back to my office. I never learned my way around the building. On top of this embarrassment, I began bringing a water bottle full of whiskey to work to keep me grounded, but I didn't worry about being caught. Often, at lunchtime, I take a nap in the car and oversleep for two hours. I figured that nobody noticed because I sure didn't.

Still, I did not recognize that the emotions in my body had piled up so high that I could not function in my job. The feeling of being tired was overwhelming my entire life.

As I continued to go to work every day, I noticed that my clothing was no longer fitting my body. In complete denial, I attributed my inability to eat to becoming more health-conscious and fit. I could not see myself as a person who was breaking. I thought other parts of my life were going well, so what could be wrong with me? Keeping myself busy with my hobbies and interests felt like a chore. Although I love social dancing and playing music, my ability to focus and concentrate on my goals waned. Part of me wanted to quit everything, and another part told myself there was no reason to leave anything because I was "fine." I had a lot to be grateful for. Even though I was trying to logic my way out of the way, I felt because that is how I made myself resilient, regular, and productive. Over time, I noticed it was impossible to be fruitful. I couldn't put my finger on it, so I just kept going on with my day, but I didn't realize that I was completely shut down because I couldn't acknowledge the pain and misery I felt around what was happening in my conscious mind. The more I tried to fill my days with work and my usual activities, the less I could do. I couldn't imagine talking to anyone about it because I couldn't think of a logical explanation for why I couldn't keep going.

I kept telling myself some people have been through far worse things, and I didn't realize it, but telling myself that there are people who go through worse things was just a way to deflect from the incident in the back of my head that was bothering me it was like trying to push a beach ball down in a pool. It kept popping up and popping up and popping until I eventually gave up. The time came at work when I would go to my desk and sit there and stare ahead at the computer. Sometimes, I would get on YouTube and try to find something funny, interesting, or scary to ensure I could still feel something. For a while, it worked, but then my work started piling up, and I would look at my stack of papers or my calendars and Do List, and I would feel heavy and tired. I was looking for a distraction from how I thought, getting old and bored. If I had my office and wondered if anybody noticed what I looked like and sounded like, I asked if my feelings were clear to the surrounding people at work. Still, I quickly reminded myself no one was paying any attention.... Or so I thought.

Summer Vacation

That summer, I took a week off to visit a friend performing and teaching at a festival in the Pacific Northwest.

I was so excited to get away, take a break from my usual surroundings, take some fresh air hiking, and visit a beautiful spa retreat resort. The only thing was I still had that unsettled feeling in my stomach because I knew I would see people who knew the abuser. Part of me wanted to tell them so badly, but I wanted to enjoy my vacation without having to relive the horror of Dad I had been going through for the past few months. When I arrived at my destination, I was ready to have fun, relax, rest, and catch up with my friends.

As the week went on, I slept extremely hard and had an even harder time waking up. Sometimes, I felt like I had slept for 16 hours but did not get enough rest. Everything around me seemed dark in my eyes. I would wake up, constantly rub my forehead, and take deep breaths. No matter how much stretching I did, my body felt like lead, and my muscles felt stiff. When I told my friend, she suggested I get a sports massage down the street. I agreed and went. This may help me. It did not help much. I was still stuck in my body with nowhere to go.

PART II: Being Sick

How I Found Out I Was Sick

In the wake of what happened to me, all I could think about was that I did not want to have to tell the story to anyone. From time to time, I would bargain with myself, saying well, maybe if I can get him to admit what he did and tell me he was on some drug I've never heard of, perhaps I could explain why this happened to me. Mentally, I felt like I would put the ball in his court so I could move on and be fine. Maybe I wouldn't have to tell on him, eventually. But what about the children? Remembering that the person teaches children, there's no telling what he could have done to them. The thought just made my skin crawl.

While these thoughts repeated, my refrigerator was full of food and beverages. Occasionally, I would mindlessly walk to the kitchen, open the fridge door, peek at all the food, and close the door. I did this for weeks. It didn't cross my mind that the food wasn't moving.

I just brushed this off and attributed it to being more emotionally fulfilled because I had a new job and a wonderful new place to live. My social life was expanding, and I was making wonderful new friends. I thought maybe it was my body's response to all the Changes in my life.

A few months later, I got a checkup at my yearly doctor's visit. My doctor mentioned that I had been losing 2 pounds weekly for the past few months and asked me what I was doing to lose weight. I said I wasn't doing anything. She said she would be pleased if I at least had some Coca-Cola and M&M's. Laughing her off, I told her I did not know why I was dropping weight but felt fine.

The following week, I saw my psychologist and psychiatrist together. As I sat across from them, I numbly explained what had happened a few months before. I wondered if my weight had something to do with that, but I figured that was ridiculous. It's not like he raped me, so there wasn't anything for me to be legitimately worried about. Thinking of myself as a strong-minded, sensible individual, I figured I must be overreacting if my weight had something to do with it.

I thought people go through much worse things, so how could I lose weight behind something that almost happened but didn't? As I told them what happened, they looked at me incredulously and asked why I hadn't told them earlier. I genuinely felt like it was over. Maybe it bothered me, but I was comparing what happened to those women in the 'Me Too' movement. This was not a big deal, and I should be just fine.

How could it be a big deal now? I told them it's been several months, and things in my life are going well, I thought. My psychiatrist asked me if I'd ever read the book The Body Keeps Score by Bessel van Cook. No, I haven't. I'm not a psychology major, so why should I have read that book? Why the hell do these doctors think I live in their fucking head? Matter-of-factly, he told me I was dropping weight because, most likely, I had PTSD from what had happened to me. He promptly sent me next door to their eating disorder specialist to talk to her about what happened. How is it that big of a deal? I thought, OK, so I dropped some weight. Maybe I'll just put down a few burgers, and I'll be back to my average weight in no time.

She is a dance therapist who specializes in treating eating disorders. Wow, I thought. I am truly on my way to the looney house and might not return. I should suspend my disbelief and listen to what she has to say because, after all, I'm the one with the alleged eating disorder, and she's probably not.

When I arrived at her office, I sat down and looked at her. Something about her warmth and kindness made me feel paranoid. Her calm and centered Yoda-type energy made me feel like I could be completely open about what happened to me, though I did not tell her immediately. I felt like a complete idiot for being there, and I hoped after our conversation, she would decide that I would be fine and could go back to work and watch YouTube for 8 hours a day. But the conversation didn't quite go as I had hoped. I waited until the last 10 minutes of our session to tack on the incident to the end because, although not that important, it might be a clue to how I was feeling.

Some part of me knew she would know exactly what to say. That just made shit too real for me to bear, and I was sure at this point that I did not want to hear it in that moment.

An enormous lump in my throat wanted to pop, but I couldn't swallow. My heart pounded so loudly that I was sure she could hear it. So, as tentatively as possible, I told her what had happened to me in the most robotic voice I could muster. "Thanks for slipping that in there at the end. Now I have a good idea of what is going on." I couldn't tell if she was being sarcastic, but I told her I felt like crying.

She said, "Then why don't you?" she said. "Because that would mean that there is something wrong. And there's nothing wrong. I'm fine." "What is wrong with there being something wrong?" She said. I couldn't answer. Feeling drained and numb, I went silent. She told me about the ED treatment center and the therapy that could help me get back into my body again. She convinced me to go to treatment, and I hesitantly and begrudgingly decided I would try it, even though I was pretty sure that this was the wrong diagnosis. An eating disorder is just a diet gone wrong, I thought. Growing up, I had seen, you know, photos on the Internet and documentaries on TV and talk shows talking about people with eating disorders and then walking around looking like skeletons.

I didn't look like a skeleton or an elephant, so why the hell are they sending me to an eating disorder clinic? That's what I thought. I am not even into dieting or a desire to be thin. I've always been a person whose height and weight are proportionate and reasonable for eating average food. They had to be wrong. Maybe I had dropped 30 lbs. In the past seven months, however, as far as I could see, I looked slightly different from what I usually do.

Can you believe that my undergarments no longer fit, resulting in me going without wearing them? I'm sure nobody else notices. I think they're just blowing all of this way out of proportion.

Starting Full-Time Treatment

When I arrived at the treatment center, they checked in and sat down across from one of their counselors, and she told me that group therapy was going on in the room next to us and that she was going to send me in there as soon as she finished my intake information. "I'm probably going to be the fattest person here," I blurted out as soon as she was talking. Without skipping a beat, she smiled and said, "That's a question about eating disorders."

The Courage to Own My Own Truth

Becoming thin is the furthest thing from my mind. I'm already skinny, and I never even think about dieting. "Eating disorders can start in a variety of ways she said. I rolled my eyes and said, I don't think it's a big deal, but my doctor said I'm no longer mentally or physically fit for work, so I'm here. At this time, I couldn't see how thin I was. I looked in the mirror and saw my body as normal, with my slightly baggy pants.

I thought, "Maybe I had some subconscious stress going on behind what had happened, but I could just start eating again. It's not that big of a deal." They told me I would be there part-time, have homework every night, and have to eat two meals on my own and the other meals with the group. When I entered the group therapy room, the girls turned and looked at me and smiled, chirping, "Hi," and waving.

It didn't cross my mind to decide what weight they were and what weight was because I felt very welcome. I had enrolled myself for part-time treatment, meaning I would have to leave work a little early to go, and I would do the regular homework, journal discussions, and exercises with my group the next day.

Thinking that when we entered treatment, we would primarily focus on food habits, I was surprised to learn that maybe 10% of our discussions centered on food. During my time there, I realized how we handled food was just a metaphor for how we took most things in life that have to do with survival and living.

Upon entering treatment, I felt even more overwhelmed. I ignored my homework and ate even less at home. After two weeks, my therapist at the clinic told me I would have to enroll in treatment full-time. I was irate. I asked her why I had to enter full-time. My condition had already improved. "Elisabeth, she said." If you feel better already, that's fine, but you're not gaining weight or doing homework. We have seen no progress in your condition in the past two weeks. The other therapists have been observing you, and we think that for you to benefit from this program and recover, you will need to be here on a full-time basis. I couldn't understand why I couldn't get it together, do homework, and eat. They seemed like such simple tasks, but I did not have the inner resources at the time to fully take part in recovery and felt like I was existing.

Two weeks into the treatment, my counselor told me I wasn't gaining any weight, nor was I doing my homework, so I would have to enroll for treatment full-time to see results. Though I had many sick days available, I was furious and frustrated with myself, thinking I should have just made myself more deep-fried okra at home, and I would not be here. At the time, I would reduce everything to a task that could or should be done. My inability to see and feel things within my body that I did not want to feel was just tricky for me. It seemed impossible. How can I tell I am not making up what I feel in my body? I wondered.

Down My mental-emotional rabbit hole- Days in Treatment

Reluctantly, I entered full-time treatment because, as the doctor put it, I was forbidden to come back to work sick. Initially, it was challenging, but I thought it would be easier. If I could treat treatment like a task that needs to be completed, I could do this. I thought I would detach and finish my meals like a person in their right mind, and I should be out of here in no time.

Since mealtimes were a part of the treatment, I passed the test and cleaned every plate I could. For days, after finishing my food, I would stare at the others as they struggled to complete the meal, feeling grateful that the therapists, who were my age, didn't have to coach me through my meals. What a relief that I'm not further embarrassing myself by staring at my plate in horror like some person who can't handle their shit, I thought. One day, a counselor asked me, "Why do you eat so fast?" What is she talking about? "I thought." "I just want to get it over with," I said. "That tells me a lot," she said. Let's slow down when you eat be present with the food, and tell me what thoughts go through your mind. As I felt myself with my meal, I could no longer finish my food. I just stopped. At that moment, I realized I could not be with food like I could not be with my emotions. I felt deeply ashamed for my inability to "get it together and take care of myself like a grown woman." How the hell did this way of thinking infiltrate my eating habits?

The Courage to Own My Own Truth

I was in group treatment or one-on-one treatment for 8 hours a day. In the morning, we would eat breakfast, enter group treatment, eat lunch, enter one-on-one treatment, have dinner, and then enter group treatment. At night, we would process everything by reviewing our homework. Some days, I would enter art therapy, and on other days, I would enter therapy with one other person who shared a similar struggle.

While in treatment, I learned that my relationship struggles started with my relationship with my emotions. I was surprised when I began exploring the connection between my emotional and physical bodies. Part of me always knew there was a connection between my emotional and physical bodies because I danced and played music. So, I positively experienced those connections that I enjoyed, but I was unaware of how I was experiencing the same connection through starving myself. To begin with, I did not think I had a severe problem. I thought to myself that I wanted to get out of treatment and get back to my normal life, so I suspended my disbelief and entertained the idea that I may have a "very" serious problem and tried to follow the rules that were given to me.

In group treatment, I observed my thinking patterns and the thinking patterns of other people who shared the same problems. It didn't matter if the person was morbidly obese or so thin that they weren't able to stand anymore; the issues we faced mainly were two sides of the same coin. I just had different ways of dealing with emotional processing. I wouldn't say I liked the phrase emotional processing, much less wanted to engage in it. It sounded like something for pussies who could not handle their shit, yet there I was, right along with everyone else who couldn't get a grip on their emotions or how they related to control.

Since I had a restrictive eating disorder, according to the therapists, restrictions were about blowing up an essential task that one needs to survive and refusing to do it to feel like one to feel like is in control of something or anything. In my mind, I didn't feel like I was blowing up any tasks; I just felt too emotionally overwhelmed to do any regular day-to-day tasks. It was hard for me to notice that my inability to acknowledge my emotions was causing physical overwhelm.

The therapists claimed I was minimizing my emotions while avoiding eating food, so I felt like I was in control of something. Other times, I would avoid going to the grocery store because I wasn't in the mood to make any decisions . It was just too hard for me to do. How could I trust myself to do anything right?

Of course, I didn't think of myself that way. I saw myself as being full of powerful emotions that made it difficult for me to eat. Either way, I believe both behaviors are entirely out of control. Neglecting decision-making was an unconscious choice. It's not something that I used to wake up and decide to starve myself. It was the overwhelming emotions I could not define nor describe that kept me from being able to do the most basic chores and tasks. I had completely lost my ability to eat, work, and sleep and did not know how to regain these abilities.

People like me, who have had anxiety about their desires to be seen, heard, and supported by those around them, often shut down their uncomfortable emotions because they believe others will not meet this desire. Unconsciously, I developed habits I thought would keep me from experiencing such situations.

The Courage to Own My Own Truth

Maybe I wouldn't apply for that job I wanted, or I would skip a meal because I had to do more "work" before taking a break. I considered these behaviors to be "reasonable." This action alone crippled my ability to experience emotions and process them. Before I knew it, food was the first thing to go, work went away, the boyfriend, hobbies, phone calls, drinks, fun, and everything else. The more I suppressed my feelings, the voice said, "You can't handle this right now; throw some dirt on it." Burying discomfort became normal for me as the voice saying "shove it" just became louder and louder until my body was completely malnourished. Still, I was sure that I could start everything back up again with no support. I thought, "Now that I knew the issue, I could bulldoze over my problems with my sharp mind." Not that simple. I did not realize it then, but staying in my mind was the worst thing I could have done for myself.

I had grown up in church, and part of me thought I had to change my beliefs about myself and my desire to be healed, not understanding then that a large part of healing is making a daily choice to accept healing.

That was part of the issue, and the other part was that I didn't know then that changing my beliefs required me to choose different behaviors regularly so that my beliefs could change. For example, sometimes I would find myself in the grocery store for an hour, unable to select over five foods to purchase. Instead of giving up on myself and leaving the store, I would phone a friend who shared a similar struggle and ask them to support me as I shopped. We didn't have to talk about food; maybe I could vent about what had recently happened that was overwhelming me, and that would create space for me to find food to eat. I found that when I changed my behaviors and saw the results I wanted, my trust in myself increased every single time.

Realizing Numbness and Unexpressed Emotions

Before and after every meal, the counselor would bring out a wheel where with around 100 emotions labeled on a circle and would ask me to identify the feelings that I was feeling in my body; often, I couldn't choose the "right" word because I did not want to be wrong. Well, that was part of it. The other part is that I was so used to suppressing the way I felt with physical or mental activities that I couldn't even describe how I felt at that moment.

I could not understand why it was so difficult to name an emotion I felt. I would sit there for some time, maybe five minutes, before I could choose the right word, and then I wondered afterward if I had picked the wrong word because I couldn't locate the feeling anywhere in my body. Emotions were words on a cardboard wheel in the therapist's office.

Over time, I blurred the lines between emotional and physical hunger. I couldn't tell the difference because I had received the message from caregivers that there were right and wrong ways to feel. The other women around me who were experiencing various eating disorders had great difficulty being able to tell the difference between emotional and physical hunger, emotional emptiness and physical emptiness, and emotional fullness and physical fullness. It was so confusing to me to have to decipher between the two because I had received the message growing up that my emotional needs were not essential and had, therefore, adopted that belief without knowing it.

The Courage to Own My Own Truth

One of the first issues I noticed was the fear of powerful emotions. For example, I never kept food that I loved in my apartment because the feeling of love for deep fried okra was just too strong for me to feel. What if the food I loved gained control over me? I thought. When powerful emotions would come, I felt uncomfortable. My inner world could not tolerate emotions; they were to be ignored, avoided, or suppressed.

When I would tune into my unexpressed emotions in treatment, it felt like a massive lump in my throat and a pressure in my chest that kept me from being able to sit up.

I eventually expressed these raw feelings as cravings for the support that I had not received when I needed it. It was the support that I had no clue how to ask for.

Feeling a sense of powerlessness over my inability to express myself the way I wanted to and needed to, I observed myself and other anorexic people as feeling emotionally empty, and binge eaters and people with bulimia felt emotionally complete. We never specifically discussed this observation in treatment because I never brought it up to anyone.

Still, I noticed the way the mind and body communicate with each other after traumatic experiences can change drastically. The only way to align my mind and body was to be physically active again.

Consciously, I noticed I had a craving for emotional expression. However, I had unconsciously turned that part of myself off because most of me was sure that the anger, frustration, and sadness weren't "helpful" in completing tasks like exercising, schoolwork, and relationships. So, I put those types of emotions on a shelf somewhere else and continued to bully myself into recovering.

The way I went about ignoring, avoiding, or suppressing discomfort and misusing food was just one way I did this. The intolerance of discomfort can overtake minds and bodies, as we see with drug addiction, alcohol, nicotine, exercise, daydreaming, sex, and porn, the rabbit hole of creating multiple "identities," "genders" working, competing, sports, tv, social media, new age, and obsessions with occult practices and the list goes on.

But when so many feelings had built up in my body, and I didn't express them through my ego, I returned to being that girl in grade school who felt unsafe in her body and longed for emotional expression. Feeling unsafe in my body after being sexually assaulted amplified my fears as I sometimes escaped into worlds I created in my mind to express such feelings. As I went through therapy, I was even more surprised that the rules I had in my mind around how and when I ate were similar to how I existed in the world. Often, I would find myself too busy or too tired to eat. This made me think I had to earn food or exhaust myself to get it. Since recovering, it's been much more accessible to discern what eating patterns reveal about my psyche and the relationship with my needs.

The Problem Around Using Food to Meet Emotional Needs

When we think of misusing food, we often think of binge eating or fad dieting to get us over a hump.

How we relate to food relates to "being" and living in the world. Food, or the lack thereof, can dictate whether we live or die or how we live and die.

People on the outside looking in often wonder what people who choose fad diets are trying to get by eating specific foods, not realizing that fad diets are a way of fulfilling emotional needs that are not being met.

Control is one of those needs people try to fulfill when they see what they perceive as some injustice in the world that they wish to see corrected.

Many of those who put themselves on a fad diet rarely know that their obsessions around "detoxing," "building strength," and feeling "clean" inside are ways to have an emotional need met. These obsessions have nothing to do with anything except that there is an emotion that is being avoided or an emotion the individual is trying to create within themselves.

Today, when I work with individuals who have food obsessions, they often feel deep shame and guilt for merely existing. Many feel that they must save animals, for example, to validate their existence, therefore feeling less guilty for existing, not knowing that they are trying to make up for the guilt they have about their emotional needs.

Another observation is that those who have suffered sexual abuse, emotional abuse, and neglect people often develop detoxing obsessions and addictions because they subconsciously feel "dirty" on the inside, not realizing that the word "dirty" is just another word for feeling human. Sometimes, we can't handle the emotional feeling of being dirty, so we try to resolve it by "cleaning out" the body.

I can relate to the feeling of disgust with my emotions, thoughts, and habits and having emotional needs that are not being met. I vilified myself for having needs and, therefore, tried to cleanse and rid my body and mind of those needs that I was "sure" could not be met.

Hating my Needs

While many of the women there had been in and out of eating disorder treatment centers throughout their lives, I was a first-timer and the oldest person there. It was an odd feeling not just to be the most senior person there but to listen to people much younger than me who had been through eating disorder treatment many times and who knew what was behind their eating disorder and why they couldn't integrate their emotions into their body.

This did not just start as an adult; I had learned these behaviors as a child and a teenager. I had come from a religious home where we were to "give our problems to God" and "move on" instead of being "controlled" by our emotions. This led to avoiding, delaying, refusing, eroding, and bulldozing needs I didn't want to have. Often I would find myself throwing myself into constant activities like volunteering and creating projects to feel productive rather than feeling my emotions. Shutting down what I called "negativity" created a cycle of exploding, looking the other way, and burying emotions I did not know how to feel and release.

Throughout my life, I have always felt discomfort expressing wants and needs out of fear of a response I don't want to get, like hearing the words no, you don't need that. As a child and teenager, I always wanted to express my feelings to my mom and dad without being shamed. I would see my friends who could express a wide range of emotions in front of their parents without being punished. I would wonder how they did it, remembering that whenever I tried to express any emotion that contradicted my parents' feelings, they would immediately punish me.

The Courage to Own My Own Truth

The punishments I received from them sent me the message to ignore my inner voice.

Growing up, I underwent many changes and hated not knowing what would happen next and jumping through many hoops to ensure everything. This only created more angst, more anxiety, more fear, and more pain than I could imagine, and I didn't even notice it.

I am the youngest child. In psychology, we hear many things about the youngest child and what they are prone to as the youngest child. In my life, people sent me the message that I would always be last in everything, so I developed the belief that I couldn't be sure of anything because I didn't know what would happen next. After the event of abuse, I experienced this intolerance of uncertainty, which only increased.

Everyone on Earth lives with uncertainty every day. Life offers no guarantees, and tomorrow is not guaranteed for anyone. But these are truths I could not sit with. I tried to escape this feeling in any way I could, and now I'd come to a place where these feelings were no longer avoidable.

They knew all the symbolic terms, the psychiatric terms, and the technical terms for what it was they were going through at such a young age. I never could explore those things when I was younger. I just assumed that if I was walking and talking, I was probably fine, not realizing that the emotions I could not integrate into my being and process had piled up so high and let me go to where everything just had to stop. I reached a point where I could no longer deny I was in serious trouble with my physical and mental health and that it was my responsibility to choose to heal and gather the pieces of myself that had scattered everywhere, like a watermelon falling from a 50-story building.

All the years of repressing and suppressing the discomfort and uncertainty of life had brought me to a place where I could no longer eat because I was full of so many unexpressed emotions that were stored in my body that I could no longer hide from. This was excruciating because I saw myself as a rigid, logical, and responsible person who was "strong" and could accomplish whatever was necessary to succeed.

The Courage to Own My Own Truth

Wondering how on Earth I could bury all these emotions and feelings for so long without exploding, then realizing the eating disorder was the explosion, I now had the choice to suspend my denial and disbelief that I had an actual diagnosable illness that was making life unbearable for me. It was surprising to realize that I did not know how to express uncomfortable emotions consciously. In therapy sessions, when I was with a counselor, they would ask me to name and convey a painful emotion; I would use words to describe it. Naming emotions did not come easily to me. It did not come because emotions were words on a page more than they were something I could locate in my body.

Other times, the rage and resentment I had in my body were so powerful that when I tried to express them through art, I would have to stop, lie flat on my back, and close my eyes. If I found I could not be able to finish a meal after expressing an uncomfortable emotion, I would mentally shame myself for hours or even days after I had failed to complete my meal. I did not want to face these extremely uncomfortable feelings of inadequacy because I could not describe how I felt, nor did I feel like exploring how the feelings got there.

PART III: The Turning Point

Exploring Gentleness

Over the next several years, I began a period of healing transformation not just around the incident of abuse but around my emotional and physical health as well. I started creating and developing inner and outer resources to support me through my transformation as I took time to relearn how to care for my physical, emotional, and spiritual bodies. Initially, I didn't understand that I had to create space to transform my relationship with myself. While contemplating my automatic responses to pain and fear, someone provided me with the tools to create space, but I didn't recognize that I could employ those tools for healing instead of merely dealing with distress.

When I talk about creating space, I'm referring to allowing my uncomfortable emotions to be there without tackling them or bombing them with everything I had. Examples of this could be harsh language, vaping, thought-stopping, drinking, binge-eating, not eating, and the list goes on.

The Courage to Own My Own Truth

When I tried to rid myself of intolerable emotions, things got worse as I noticed I was piling on judgments about everything I did. After I learned to change the way I related to my feelings, how I approached learning anything wholly changed. I made some of the changes without even consciously realizing it. For example, during my fourth month of treatment, I went to the skating rink for fun. Not having been to the rink for several years, I wanted to dance around, move my body, and have some fun.

I tried to land a few jumps I had not tried in years. Singles and doubles. Not only did I land them quickly, but I also landed them without fear of what I looked like. This was huge for me. Where was the voice? My mind felt so free from the harsh voices that had plagued my psyche and affected how I approached everything. I sat down with my skates on and cried in a corner of the rink. Where was all of this when I was younger? Thinking I was just a defective person who needed to try harder than everyone else, I always thought that if I adopted rigorous routines and stuck with them, I could at least live with myself, knowing that I tried as hard as possible.

At least I maintained discipline and commitment to improve constantly. Many aspects of me benefited from this type of thinking. I realized that developing patience with myself would help me even more than the routines did and that if I could extend myself some compassion, I could make more significant gains. Opening up to my teachers about my fears and doubts gave my practices more depth and less fear around what I believed was possible. Today, when I talk to people involved in the same type of pursuits who share the same love and passion for artistic pursuits, many of them also feel the same way I did.

I'm learning now that the more I open up about my struggles, the less power my parts that don't believe what I can accomplish have in my life.

Fear of Seeking Support

In the past, as a child and a teenager, I always saw asking for help as pointless. I feared asking for help because I was never sure I would get it, even if it was from my parents. I was always told what I needed, what I could need or desire, and what to do.

The Courage to Own My Own Truth

While growing up, I never received instructions to express my needs or desires clearly, so I learned to stay silent and care for them independently. While there is nothing wrong with doing things ourselves, we should remember that there are certain things we should not attempt alone. I used not to know the difference between the two, thinking that if I were to accomplish something or move past something painful, I would have to do it alone no matter what.

When the feeling of "weakness" came over me, I learned to "figure it out" on my own by adding more shame to situations that I thought I "shouldn't be in, thinking that if I berated myself enough that I would get my shit together.

The incident of sexual abuse that I suffered only brought back these feelings stronger than I could have ever imagined.

If I didn't place as highly in a competition as I had wished, I would wonder what was wrong rather than notice how much I had improved. I thought I could be more intelligent, stronger, faster, and better.

For me, asking for support was something that made my stomach queasy. I often thought: What if I'm not worth it, and everyone can tell? My parents sure can tell that my gifts and talents do not matter. Still, some part of me knew that my gifts and talents did matter because I willingly accepted help when it was offered to me. Even if I still felt that I wouldn't get help, I learned that people around me were happy to provide support if I reached out for help; with enthusiasm and passion, I pursued to improve my hobbies and work. Before the incident of abuse, I did not realize how loved I was by the surrounding people. I figured some were just around me because we loved the same things. That wasn't true. I had friends and teachers around me who were there because they loved me. Now, I understand that the most significant sign of healing I have witnessed in myself is the ability to ask for help when I need it and accept the help I am offered.

Even though I was Mistreated My Gifts Still Matter

As a child, I remember telling my parents that I wanted to work in certain professions because I wanted a joyous reaction from them.

If I told them I wanted certain things, they would accept me for who they wanted me to be, not knowing I was betraying who I was. They didn't assure me they would support my gifts and talents without question, and they told me they would if I obediently honored my parents. There was a fitting way to feel and a wrong way to feel about everything.

If I could talk to my younger self, I would tell her several things that would make a transformation in all areas of life more manageable. First, I would tell my younger self to resist judging yourself for how you merely feel.

When I would find myself grieving over the person I was before I was attacked, I would hate myself for even feeling grief. Often, I canceled my plans to go to concerts or spend time with a friend because I was wrestling with heaviness and shame over not being positive enough. Facing the fact that my abuser had treated me the same way my family had was an awful but truthful realization that I could not sit with.

The fact that I was being treated like I did not matter was excruciating. Other times I would sit in a bathtub for an hour and binge watch my favorite movies while drinking my feelings away hoping that I would feel cleaner and more relaxed afterwards.

It takes practice and is a challenging feat for many of us. Many of us find it difficult to access the parts of ourselves that could be strengthened during times of frustration and disappointment because of distractions like social media, food, drinks, etc. Nowadays, when I want to engage in distractions, I put my phone down and look at a blank wall for five minutes. I learned this practice from a psychologist who told me it would help me go within for strength. This practice has changed how I relate to my mind in ways I never imagined.

Becoming Aware of Self-Abandonment

Realizing the patterns, cycles, and behaviors that surrounded my struggles is a part of me that is constantly evolving because I have realized and developed as I notice and accept what I struggle with.

For me there was much confusion over what I could and could and could not control in my life.

I allow all thoughts and feelings, even if they are uncomfortable, to be there without trying to judge or change them for a while. This is not easy if you believe that "negative" feelings must be stopped or "fixed."

Second, people are comprised of multiple parts, and only some of our parts will always align with what we desire to be. I remember pressuring myself into checking as many "boxes" as possible in order to correct how I felt.

I've found that being "right" or having to get it "right" creates confusion around what is precisely suitable for me. I've started thinking in terms of what is best for me right now instead of trying to live in the future. It is tempting always to ask myself what if this or that happens to me? This could not have happened had I not chosen to do something I would not have considered, like seeking professional help. Again, I accepted the support my soul had been aching for. It was extremely difficult for me,

As I learn to radically accept where I am right now is to remember that the person I am in this incarnation, in this time, in this place, and in this body is who I am. There are things I am currently capable of, and there are things I will never be capable of. The question arises: Do I want to be honest with myself? Will you make myself or others "wrong" for not getting everything "right?"

After Self Abandonment-Creating Space for My Hated Parts

How do you create space for those parts of you that you hate so much just to be there?

It's difficult to stop and resist the urge to feed the hatred. In my process of transformation, I struggled with allowing the hatred to be there without trying to get rid of it. Continually engaging with people who loved me for all of my perceived and fundamental flaws and distortions and communicating the parts I was disgusted by helped me. Realizing that the parts I hated weren't all of me was a big deal. I think that so many times, I would make a powerful statement about a part of myself, thinking that because that one part was so loud, it was all of me. Nothing could have been further from the truth.

Those parts were just parts that needed to be acknowledged and then put in their places. Learning about those parts, who they were, and why they were there was a significant step for me in understanding that I did not have to eliminate or berate the parts to be successful in whatever task I was undertaking.

Then the next question arises: Will I consciously give the parts I hate a chance to express themselves so that I can tell them where their place is? Can I let the parts you hate lead? Will I help the parts that love me guide me as you to the truth?

In today's Self-Help world, we are often told to "celebrate" and defend the self-destructive parts of ourselves by practicing "acceptance." I learned that acceptance is not about defending where or who you are. Acceptance is about realizing where I am now and that I can take steps to change the parts of me that seek to abuse myself or hurt others when I am feeling alone or inadequate. When I accepted my humanity, overwhelm, fear, and disgust, I could see more clearly where they came from and why asking for support in developing and cultivating the inner resources was acceptable. I needed to make those changes, one by one even if it was painful at times.

Some of the changes that came to my mind as I stared at a white wall the truth came up because some of me knew I could take steps to make the changes I needed. It would not come to my mind if we couldn't make the changes. Making changes simultaneously will not happen because humans are not designed that way. Growing up, I was told to decide based on what was moral, right, and sensible. No one ever said that significant life decisions relate to emotional alignment. I was always told not to let my emotions "control" me. No one had informed me that humans make the most important life decisions not by logic but by the emotional experiences they desire. It's not right or wrong to choose this way, but it is wise to look deeper into why we want to experience the things we choose to experience.

As a coach, I refuse to tell people they can "be anything they want" because many often unknowingly want to betray who they are for the meaning they attach to becoming someone they will never and could never be in their complete authenticity.

Oftentimes, I did not realize that being who I wanted to be involved in doing things that felt terrible at the time would get me where I wanted to be. The word sacrifice comes to mind when I think of people "being anything they want."

We force ourselves into professions, wanting what we think is behind the titles and accolades, telling ourselves that we want to be medical doctors, attorneys, engineers, influencers, singers, actors, thin, thick, etcetera because that would mean "I'm smart," "I'm beautiful," or "I'm right." When we ask ourselves, "Why Do I want this thing?" "Why do I want to have this experience?" What would having this experience or doing this thing mean to me?

Then, find out by answering these questions what our emotional needs are. Our emotional needs are often tied to our gifts and talents and what we are good at, but we are too afraid to go in that direction because it does not always seem rational.

So, the question remains: Do I want to have that one thing or experience? Or do I like what I think is behind it? Is it adoration and respect to be seen as "smart," "talented," or "beautiful" that I want? Or is this my true-life path?

Self-abandonment can take many forms, and what I just spoke of is only one of them. After the incident of sexual abuse, I abandoned myself when I needed to care for myself the most because that is what I learned to do to cope with how I felt.

When we remember that there are parts of us that can aid us in making transformations in how we relate to our bodies and how we relate to humanity, to demand help and support from certain parts of yourself that you aren't currently capable of loving is asking for water from a dry well. My life changed when I learned to ask the parts of me that believe I can use my gifts and talents to support me physically, spiritually, and emotionally.

In this current anxiety-ridden world, self-judgment and the judgment of others precipitate people's fears and doubts without understanding all the "parts" of ourselves, others, and situations we come across.

The Courage to Own My Own Truth

Learning that my habit of self abandonment came from mistreating the parts of myself that aren't aligning with what I thought I should want to be, have, and do was huge for me. Instead of mistreating the parts of myself that I could not stand, or maybe even hated, I have learned to let those parts exist and have a voice, but not let my hatred for those parts lead the way in any area of my life. It's a practice that I must constantly remind myself of as I develop wisdom to discern what needs to come next. Today, there is a lot of confusion about what to do with "negativity." I do not believe in negative emotions or positive emotions. Some emotions are just more comfortable than others. It's possible to be more comfortable with rage rather than joy because emotions we are more comfortable expressing often make us feel seen and heard. Other times, we are more comfortable with emotions that make us feel invisible, depending on what creates more safety. Either way, regarding the more powerful emotions, it can be highly uncomfortable if you are used to being punished or receiving a surplus of unwanted attention. Recently, it has become easier to distinguish when I am trying to avoid the less comfortable emotions and what helps me process them.

Reclaiming My Body

As I develop the strength, awareness, and wisdom to say yes, "That's right for me," or "No, that's wrong for me," I have developed more trust in myself to stand up for all of myself, even the parts I dislike or even hate.

Another central turning point in my healing journey came after I finished my time in treatment when I made an appointment with the counselor who had initially seen me when I was working at my job. I told her I still had somewhere the gift my abuser had given me, but I did not know where it was since I had moved to my new place. She asked me why I still had it. I told her I didn't think it mattered. She told me to dig through my belongings, find them, and put them where I could see them daily. I asked her why. She said to do it and decide at the end of the week how seeing the gift made me feel. So, I did it. Passing by the gift every day for a week, covering my face, I felt my stomach churning. I could not take the feeling of disgust and fury anymore. Why did I keep it? I wondered. Was I trying to prove to myself that what had happened didn't matter? Then I realized I buried the gift like I was constantly burying emotions in what happened.

At the end of the week, I felt irritated, ashamed, and gross. I grabbed the gift, tore it into a thousand pieces, and burned it outside. At that moment, overwhelmed with power, I informed the relevant authorities about the abuse that I and others had suffered at the hands of this individual. I did not doubt in my mind that I could tell my story.

Around the same time I told my story, my dear friend, Jean Dorff, and dance coach opened up to me about his experience of abuse at the hands of a family member. As he informed me, he intended to share his story by writing a book about it. He was nervous about it, but knew it was a story that needed to be told. He told me he knew that telling his story might anger some people he loved, but God led him to tell it. I was in complete awe at his bravery and thought I could never do such a thing. What would his family think? He had never told his father and mother, just like I had never told mine. How could he be so brave? He told me that the ego does not want us to share these types of stories but that when we remove our ego and decide that taking action to heal ourselves and others is more important, we can be free.

I received so much inspiration from Jean that I entertained the idea of telling my story to someone who could do something about what happened to me. Then I dreamed. In my dreams at night, a few of the people I knew who also knew my abuser came to me in the dream and told me they knew what he was doing to people and that I should meet with them in person and tell them what he did to me.

Not only did I find it shocking to have dreams, but I also surprised myself by believing I needed to tell them when I woke up.

Deep down inside, I knew they knew something about this person and that it was safe to tell them everything.

The Turning Point-Deciding to Report Abuser

After making a few phone calls to meet with the people who could punish my abuser, I felt like I could fly. The pure joy from standing in my power flooded my entire body. Every part of my being felt light and free from shame and despair. As I sat down and told them what happened, to my surprise, they believed me and offered support for sharing my story.

I remember asking myself, "Why couldn't I have told my story like this earlier? I could have freed myself so much sooner had I mustered the courage. Why was I so weak before? Why couldn't I have been stronger than you? What is so different from who I am now? I did not know the enormity of finally speaking up for myself and being seen and heard by someone who could act on what had happened to me.

PART IV: The Transformation

The Importance of Creating Space for Transformation

When my transformation started, I didn't even know it. In one way, doctors forced me to undergo treatment. Still, in another way, I will suspend my disbelief that I had a severe problem and allow my mind to be open to the fact that I could challenge some of my current beliefs about how I saw myself, how I related to my emotions, and how I related to others because of my learned ways of thinking and being in the world. Few people could stop working and spend 40 hours a week in therapy for six months, dismantling their belief systems and ways of relating to their emotions. It was a blessing to do so, even though it was not my idea to go. What I realized is that it took a lot for me to decide to enter treatment and suspend some beliefs that I had held for so long that I thought were keeping me safe.

In the diet, I thought of myself as rational, capable of getting the job done and doing my best, all while keeping the perfect attitude type of person, not realizing that feeling good and always keeping the right attitude no matter what was happening could hurt me. Unbeknownst to me, the way I expressed my emotions was preventing me from achieving my long-held desires, and the only thing that indeed held my attention was enduring the traumatic experience of abuse.

I'm unsure if I would have ever realized how I related to my emotions on such a deep level if it hadn't happened.

I'm not one of those idiots who says everything happens for a reason, because I just don't believe that. What I think is how we respond to the problematic situations that arise in our lives can be a determining factor in whether we live or die. It could be a physical death, or it could be a spiritual death. It could be the death of our hopes and dreams, but she's if we do not take the time to learn that our emotions can speak to us and that we can have certain emotions without casting judgment upon ourselves for merely having a feeling.

The Courage to Own My Own Truth

Now, I'm a person who believes that with any emotion that comes up, it's essential to ask yourself what the emotion that I'm feeling is and allow it to be there without judging yourself for having an uncomfortable or confusing emotion. Growing up, I was told that if you're feeling anger or resentment, you must repent because you are bad. Unfortunately, I took this into my adult life and practiced that belief until I didn't know who I was or where I was anymore. I was a person who completely dissociated from uncomfortable emotions because I wouldn't say I liked the feeling.

I thought if I was to feel anger, hatred, or resentment, then it must mean that there was something wrong with me, and I was the last person on earth who wanted there to be something wrong with me or anything, for that matter.

Now I know that to create space for transformation, I have to acknowledge that I'm feeling something that I don't want to feel and that there's nothing wrong with a feeling, but how I relate to it determines my mental and emotional health. I've learned that denying my humanity is a type of emotional self-harm and that if I had continued, then I literally could have been physically dead. Today, people have all kinds of coping mechanisms and strategies to beat themselves into what they think is good and just.

An example is when people on television or the Internet take sides and actively engage in saying and doing things to others that they would never want to happen to them or never want to be said to them. People make demands of others, asking for things that don't exist in this plane of reality to meet their emotional needs. Many of these people don't know that they are abusing the people around them or trying to act in retribution upon people they don't even know to have an emotional need met. They get on the Internet and tell others that their emotions and the foods they choose to eat determine if they are Adolf Hitler or not. While it's not always this extreme, it's important to remember that people do to others what they do to themselves.

I can remember when I would go into the grocery store and see a person who is larger than a Ford F350 truck with ice cream and frozen pizza in their buggy and wonder when they would die. Now, I look at them with compassion and wonder what could have happened to them. They could have been looking at me when I was at my lowest weight and wondered when I was going to die. You can accept your power to meet your emotional needs without abusing others, including Adolf Hitler's name and everything that comes with it.

Exploring the Pain of Self-Care

Reporting the abuser was just the beginning of my transformation. I realized other parts of myself as I learned to speak up for myself. Issues around control often arose as I observed my awareness and thoughts about my state of being in the world. In the past, I have not always understood what was in my control and what was not.

The deeper we go into technology and the deeper we go into the human brain and thought, the more confusing it can seem to understand what's in our control and what's out of our control.

I used to believe that the more awareness I had about how my mind works, the easier it would be to change my behaviors. That is one component of the equation, and the other part is practicing self-care, which is a confusing topic in the self-help world. When people hear "self-help," they usually think of de-stressing, slowing down, or taming their monkey minds.

Some corners of the "self-help" world often define activities like exercise, journaling, bubble baths, meditation, mirror work, affirmations, subliminal recordings, coloring books, etc., as being self-care activities.

While the aforementioned activities can help individuals de-stress or target mental and emotional struggles, I do not think of those activities as self-care. I define self-care as changing my usual responses to my usual struggles. When done right, this can be very scary and disorienting because we are setting a boundary with ourselves that we have not set before. An example of this would be to stand up for oneself as an act of self-care. For example, when one stands up to an abusive colleague when it's not usually something one would do at work, it can be both frightening and relieving at the same time.

The Courage to Own My Own Truth

On the one hand, you couldexperience conflict because of standing up for yourself and being completely authentic, and you can feel empowered to speak up for yourself in the future and not just at work. The effects of speaking up for ourselves can create peace in the parts of us that are not used to experiencing peace. This may not always feel "good" because in the past, we may have unknowingly prioritized "keeping peace" for others while losing ourselves in resentment and anger. I found that obsessing over my thoughts and trying to control them only brought more resentment I had towards the powerful emotions that overwhelmed me.

For many people like me, choosing different responses and behaviors is the most beneficial way to change what keeps me from operating authentically with myself and others. Changing responses is not always the easiest thing to do because I believed my thoughts and responses kept me safe from experiencing things I did not want to experience, like frustration and anger with people I cared about. Now that I have allowed myself to stop making other people feel comfortable, I can look in the mirror and appreciate myself for letting others experience how I feel, too.

Getting Good at Doing Nothing

As a coach, people often ask me how they can be more productive. Maybe they have an addiction to doom scrolling or other distractions. Since I struggled with distractions, I earned a Ph.D. in Distractions and Obsession Sciences, and they rescinded the degree when I discovered I could train my brain to enjoy focusing on one thing at a time. First, let's go into how and why distractions and obsessions exist. I developed obsessions and distractions because I wanted to avoid feelings that made me uncomfortable. Like many people, I did not enjoy facing certain tasks and specific situations and feeling like I didn't know what would come next. So, I use distractions to give me something else to think about or figure out primarily things that have nothing to do with me to make myself feel like I was doing something important. Well, you may not have ever had an eating disorder or an obsession with always getting it right or getting it perfect. You may feel overwhelmed by dismantling the things in your life, like harmful belief systems

They are in place, but you can't quite define what they are, so you distract yourself from figuring it out because it's too complex and confusing. That's where we get more comfortable being

After what happened to me, I noticed the habits and beliefs around my mental, physical, and spiritual well-being keep me from processing emotions stuck in my body. Studying, learning, and practicing what I enjoyed were often used to distract me from processing the pain and discomfort I was in. A lot of the avoidance increased and intensified after my incident of sexual abuse because I was still trying to protect myself from the feelings of being in danger.

I picked up a book, watched the internet, or rehearsed a dance to avoid thoughts I did not want to have so automatically that I didn't realize what I was doing to avoid the emotions and thoughts that went along with deep denial.

Even though I had the tools to handle and manage the eating disorder, no one had talked to me about my daily habits and how they were affecting the way I showed up for myself.

I didn't realize it then, but when I constantly took in new information to numb my feelings about what happened, I did not have enough time to be alone with my thoughts and feelings, and I could not notice any other external influences.

As I opened myself up to examining what was happening when I would have automatic responses, I realized I needed to remove the distractions to get in touch with what I was experiencing in those moments. When I removed social media from my phone, I tapered down on the wine and vaped substantially without even attempting to.

Removing distractions allowed me to listen to my intuition again and trust what it told me about what I needed and how to approach healing. If you had asked me a few years ago if I thought my habits were keeping me from processing my thoughts, emotions, actions, and behaviors, I would have said no because I don't like being bored. I'm realizing that what I call "boredom" is space. I now know I can open space without stepping over my heart. Reducing the surrounding distractions has enabled me to focus on things that need my attention and develop clarity around my values and the people I care about most.

The Courage to Own My Own Truth

The beauty of clarity lies in my ability to witness resilience erupt within my psyche, saying, "You can experience these terrible things, process them, and emerge healed on the other side." You don't have to suppress these feelings anymore. You are not less of a vital person if you cry in grief or mourn the person you once were. Everything in life is cyclical, and if you can accept support as you go through the cycles and changes in life, you can strengthen others and yourself.

As a coach, I noticed that many people today struggle with the same issues around distractions when creating space for transformation. They don't even know how much the constant activity keeps them from noticing their emotions, thoughts, and life path. I remember when I often believed that constant activity was just a part of who I was and that the things I was doing were very passionate about. I didn't realize how I was using my hobbies and the things I loved to distract myself from the things I felt I could not handle. Today, I let the things I love bring me back to a sense of presence and power within myself by letting myself be with my creativity.

Even though I still enjoy learning to play new music, I have learned to acknowledge my strength and power as often as I notice weakness and feel overwhelmed. If I can handle one, I can feel the other. I used to believe that balance was about creating balance between activities. That is one balance: it's not the most essential. I've learned that the most crucial balance is slowing down and acknowledging uncomfortable emotions with the same intensity and enthusiasm that we accept and recognizing the feelings we are more comfortable with or at home.

Giving myself the space to understand the spiritual aspects of transformation has been one of the more complex and exciting parts of my life. The most eye-opening part of understanding the spiritual aspects of creating space has a lot more to do with realizing that a higher power is always here with me and that he communicates with me in ways that I wouldn't expect God to communicate. I think that often when we think of the voice of God; we think of some deep voice coming out of the sky telling us precisely what to do next in a highly threatening and dramatic way.

The Courage to Own My Own Truth

I've learned that when I take the time to silence my mind, listen to my guidance, and align our wills with God's, he will speak to us through people's signs and experiences. If we align ourselves enough with our higher selves or inner voices, we will realize what God has to share with us and know how to apply what he says to our daily lives.

I've found that I am more creative with finding healthy ways to express my emotions when I'm not surrounded by distractions and activities that have nothing to do with going to the places I want to go and experiencing the things I want to share. As a coach, I often come across people who fill their calendars with endless activities because they want to experience the feeling of being productive, not knowing that many of the things they're involved with may temporarily give them the sense of doing what they are "supposed to" be doing.

Constant motion is an addiction many people today have fallen prey to because they spend so much time filling their minds with the emotions and feelings of the media and people around them that they don't give themselves a chance to hear their inner voice.

We stay on a treadmill of endless mental or physical activity, not knowing why we are involved in those activities and thinking that we are doing what we "should" be doing.

These days, I have a notebook and a whiteboard with a list of the activities I want to apply myself in, why I involve myself in those activities, and what I hope to gain and give to myself and others. The firm belief is that it's essential to know why I involve myself in certain activities and to understand the emotional component that comes with it, because it's necessary to have an emotional connection to what I'm involved in. I also give myself time alone to play beautiful music that speaks to me and makes me feel good before bed.

Filling my days with long periods of silence and meditation has done so much for my ability to refocus on things I want for myself and other people who have gone through similar experiences that I have had. Space is beautiful to experience when I want to hear my inner voice. I don't have to apologize for seeing the truth in my heart as I build trust with my inner guidance.

I must cultivate the discipline of building trust in myself daily. It's a choice to relieve myself from all the other voices that tell me what I must do to receive the peace I seek. Receiving peace and power through the discipline of acceptance and love for all the parts I'm unsure of and don't align with what I desire is a winding road and a journey to discovering who I truly am.

The Practice of Connection with Other People

I have always loved being a person who loves socializing, talking, and being with people. Meeting new friends and acquaintances has always been easy because I love being part of social and volunteer groups with people sharing my joys and passions.

The Courage to Own My Own Truth

Before my transformation, I did not know precisely how to connect with the parts of myself that I did not feel comfortable with. Learning to communicate with all of me was not something I practiced regularly because I was afraid to face my sadness, rage, pain, and feelings of helplessness. They would never subside if I got in touch with all these emotions. What I learned is that the opposite is the truth. Today, as I give myself opportunities to feel, I have more opportunities to heal. Now that I am conscious of how I respond to my emotions, I regularly find creative ways to express myself so that I'm not taking my anger out on others, nor am I taking things out on myself. It can be as simple as calling a friend or drawing out what I connect with on paper. Often, I surprise myself with what comes out because I cannot always express what I am experiencing, but my strength lies in allowing all of it to be there, even the parts that I do not fully understand.

Connecting and spending time with women and men who look for the good in others and celebrate each other's successes has become an integral part of my life.

I have always found that connecting with people who share the same interests and celebrate each other's successes makes my life something to look forward to.

Exploring Discipline

My daily life has changed since my transformation. Today, I know all my mental, physical, and emotional bodies. While I cannot claim that I'm always comfortable experiencing my emotions and thoughts in their fullness, I can confidently say that I have become someone who can check in with myself and acknowledge how I feel, limiting the surrounding judgments.

Still, I struggle to understand physical hunger cues. However, I know I avoid emotion when choosing what to eat, which takes forever and a day. Realizing these types of responses to stress and my eating habits has helped me understand how I relate to my feelings and what to do about them. Years ago, I would have never thought these two things had anything to do with each other. I would have told you it is just a matter of mind over matter and that food is just food.

Now I know that what keeps us alive (food) is just a metaphor for life. I can choose life, or I can choose death. It is not just a physical death I'm choosing; it's the death of accepting my gifts, the death of all of my emotions, not just the uncomfortable ones, and the death of the courage to face my fears, hopes, and doubts.

Recently, I did not know that even discipline was an emotion. I thought that discipline was an attribute that had to be developed through sheer will. While "discipline" can sound severe, developing discipline leads to the happiness we seek. By cultivating this emotion, I have discovered that I can accomplish so much in the physical, emotional, and spiritual realms for my benefit and the benefit of others, along with patience.

I had no clue that for me to discipline myself to improve my mental and physical health, I would have to allow myself to feel pain the same way I could feel the joy of letting the emotion of discipline be present in my life. When we go to concerts and performances and see artists who can bring out emotions in their audiences, we experience the results of discipline and patience.

For me, it's exhilarating to have the experience of listening to a live performance and have a sense of integration afterward. Most people don't know what they are experiencing when this happens, but I have experienced this many times.

Meditation

Meditation has gained much more popularity in the past 20 years, and I am thankful for that. There are so many types of meditation that it would be impossible for me to mention them all in this book. There's a lot of talk about meditation. Still, I've decided that if you don't have any reason for doing it other than someone else suggesting it, you may not find a reason to make meditation a habit.

Like many people, when I started meditation, I found it extremely difficult and irritating because I felt like I wasn't producing anything other than anxiousness. If it wasn't bad enough to sit still for over five minutes, sitting still for over five minutes without evaluating, analyzing, and fixing was torture. Sometimes, I wondered if something was wrong with me because my mind would bounce everywhere, so, at my doctor's prompting, I started meditating by staring at a blank wall.

The Courage to Own My Own Truth

This practice enabled me to understand so much about my obsessions and distractions. Meditating daily has helped me notice when I am touching my phone and see why I am reaching for it. My behaviors feel so deliberate and conscious now that I experience time entirely differently.

Whether it's a guided meditation or just sitting with my breath, I can notice which parts of me, both physical and mental issues, need attention and care.

I believe that discipline has helped me explore presence and develop an awareness of what I am aligning myself with. There is so much going on in our minds on a conscious and subconscious level that we are unaware of.

Meditation aids me in allowing myself to accept not just my humanity but also my ability to develop trust in my intuition for caring for myself. These are all things that I had to relearn after the trauma I experienced. There are so many things that trauma can disrupt for communicating with our spiritual, mental, and emotional bodies. Contracting Anorexia was how my body was trying to communicate with me, telling me that every other part of me was going to pieces.

While I have struggled with anxiety disorders all my adult life and tried to get rid of them, I never understood that acknowledging and accepting their presence in my life would lead me to develop the ability to lessen their impact on my life. I have spent so much time suppressing things I did not want to experience because of the feelings they gave me. Now, if I choose, I have tools like meditation that can aid me in connecting with my parts without obsessing over emotions like shame, disgust, and doubt. If someone had told me before the incident of abuse that the only way out is through emotions, I would have asked, "Why should I let 'negative' emotions control me? I can do better than that."

Writing and playing music

Writing regularly has enabled me to give all of me a voice. Even when I am not writing for others to read, I can safely express myself without fear of judgment from others...even me. I've found that when I write regularly, I find myself less involved in distractions to suppress emotions. I enjoyed writing in grade and high school, which I did freely and creatively until I entered college.

Now that I am writing again, I see writing to speak to others and validate my emotions with compassion and truth. Something so powerful about putting pen to paper or dictating into the computer makes the parts of me feel seen and heard by myself and know others whom I can help. It's vital for me to engage in creative pursuits and express myself how I choose to do it daily. Even if I only have five minutes a day, I take a little time to experience an awareness of my talents and the things that light up my life. I regularly attend live music performances at the symphony, opera, and performance halls with people who share my love for music. There is something so unique and exhilarating about sharing the same space with sometimes centuries-old music or being able to make-believe with the characters on stage and being so grateful after sharing the experience with such gifted, disciplined, and beautiful artists.

Showing my support for those who enrich society is always a tremendous honor.

Key Lesson: Acceptance

When I look back at what happened to me, there are a few things that I would tell myself about how to handle an incident of sexual abuse.

What first came to me in the upcoming days and the weeks and months after the incident was, well, the person didn't rape you, so you should be fine. Another prominent thought was that some people have been through much worse things. Why am I blowing this up in my head so much? I genuinely believe that my inability to acknowledge what had happened to me was not just because of my background and the way I usually handled painful experiences; I think that the way I took it had a lot to do with the way I compared myself to other people's experiences around me instead of just looking at how I felt about what had happened to me.

My inability to acknowledge what happened to me ended up causing me to compound blow-up issues that were already brewing under the surface from past hurts.

On the one hand, I wanted an apology from my abuser, and I wanted him to admit that what he did was wrong for me to move on. I judged myself for wanting to depend on what he did for me to heal.

The Courage to Own My Own Truth

I know for a fact that many people feel the same way whenever they have experienced an incident of abuse, whether it be one incident or multiple incidents.

When the abuse stops, they want the other person or people to apologize or make up for what they did to them, sometimes knowing that the other person is sick and evil and that they cannot admit what they did. I realized it is up to me to choose to heal daily for my sake. I can choose to heal whether the other person who attacked me is sorry or not.

I think I deflected a lot of what happened to me because I didn't want to admit how embarrassed I was and how much pain I was in after it had happened. I'm not just a person who doesn't enjoy being in pain or talking about being in pain; I am just a person who just avoided receiving or experiencing pain or conflicts of any kind, but after the incident, I could no longer ignore not just what had happened to me but up to that point how I had treated myself when I was in pain and other situations as well. I'm not happy that I went through that terrible experience. Still, I am glad that I learned in the 12 months that followed how I manage my emotions and practice healthy ways of being in the world.

I realized I could learn how to manage my emotions and relate to my feelings without hurting myself or anyone else. It's not always possible to hurt myself emotionally. Still, it is possible to make amends with the parts of me I wouldn't say I like when I notice that healing is always available for me if I choose it. Healing sounds like a logical choice. However, it's not a simple choice because we all have so many wounds we accumulate from childhood, our teenage hood, and adulthood that can sometimes seem impossible to heal. I remember at 18 that I had accumulated wounds I wasn't even aware of.

No matter your sex, ethnicity, culture, or religious background, your healing methods will differ depending on how you want to give your pain a voice and take steps to show yourself compassion so that you can be open to the idea that you are in complete control of making the difficult choice to be available to change your way of being. When first introduced to the word compassion, I always thought of compassion as self-pity. Growing up, I was told never to feel sorry for myself, no matter the circumstance, because there was a way out.

I assumed that ignoring how I felt and just moving on, not knowing that to move on, I would have to acknowledge that the way I felt was just a part of being human. As a person who has wrestled with disordered eating patterns and PTSD, I already felt like there was too much wrong with me for me to stop and acknowledge that what I was going through was not only extremely common but the things that I went through were just a part of the human experience. I often wondered why, when I was trying to do my best, all these things were happening to me. Now I know that the things that happened to me are just a part of the larger picture of understanding myself as a profoundly flawed and perfectly human individual.

I often wondered if I was doing all the things that I thought I should do to the best of my ability and why isn't everything working out how I had pictured in my mind, not realizing that my focus was on what was going wrong rather than seeing that some things went well. Some things were completely out of my control. I think that as I struggled with perfectionistic thinking.

Playing Jenga with Myself—Getting in Touch with Pain, then Rage

In the past, I was afraid to get in touch with rage. I only let rage come out once a year; not everything usually gets broken. Sometimes, I would lose a friendship because of it. If I could do some things over, I would tell myself that getting in touch with rage is just as important as love. Growing up, I had said to myself that the emotions of anger and rage were not the right emotions to feel. I thought that if I could put those emotions away and feel positivity and look on the bright side of everything, then that would mean that I was spiritually intact, not knowing at the time that if I allowed the shame around feeling anger and rage to dominate my thoughts, actions, and decisions. I did not know that shame and confusion overshadowed my expression and my inability to accept what had happened to me and how I felt about it. Getting in touch with rage came out only a few times per year for me.

Whether I was beating my computer with a hammer, slamming my fist on a printer that wouldn't print, or screaming at someone who asked me to repeat myself, rage made me feel alive. In the past, I was afraid of expressing rage because I was unsure what to do next, but now I see expressing rage as a part of being human. There's no longer any reason for me to fear rage or think it is wrong to express anger.

Abandoning the Self

Now I know that manipulating my thoughts and feelings for the sake of not wanting to feel anything terrible was not only un-authentic, but it was also detrimental to my health. I did not know that I could allow myself to handle all the emotions that come along with being wronged, abused, and misguided and not beat myself up for being screwed up. Today, in my relationship with myself, there is so much power and acknowledgment of how I feel without judging or trying to get rid of it. I have let emotions pass through my body, knowing I will not always feel them if I allow them to be handled. In the self-help community, there's much talk about changing your thoughts to change your behaviors.

But I don't think people don't understand that your thoughts come from your body, not your mind. If you had told me that my thoughts and my feelings were coming from my body and not my mind, I would have said that you were some new-age delusional joke. When I realized that the thoughts I had about myself were coming from my body and not my mind, I realized the pain from my wounds was leading me to think in ways that destroyed my entire being, and I did not notice it. The traumas I suffered had infiltrated every part of me by distorting my thoughts and how I treated my body.

I was starving myself not just physically, but I was starving the parts of me that needed to be seen, heard, supported, and understood.

When I started working with a coach the year after the incident of abuse, I learned that shaming myself for feeling the wrong way was key, preventing me from obtaining not just the peace that I wanted in my life but shaming myself for just being a human being kept me from being completely authentic with myself and others.

Today, I found creative ways to express myself and my emotions, and it's still a learning process for me because for me to engage with expression, I must face the feelings and thoughts that bring heaviness to my spirit.

Learning to express uncomfortable emotions as an adult has been no easy feat because I still struggle with expressing emotions that I strongly dislike; however, as I practice letting them be there, it's so much easier for me to move on to the next thing when I make amends with myself for mistreating the parts of me I don't like. How do I make amends with myself, you ask? Acknowledge and accept how I feel and do nothing about it. So often, I wanted to rush and "fix" what I was thinking and feeling without even noticing what I was trying to "fix," not noticing that avoiding facing the disgust I had for myself was occurring under the surface.

For a long time, I believed that what I did was who I was. The question of being versus doing was something I needed to learn the difference between. Like so many people, I equated "productivity" and reaching my goals to "success," not knowing that every step I took towards authenticity and acceptance was a victory.

Coaching

If you had asked me when I was in college what I would do in five years, I would have said I had no clue. I was in survival mode for so long that I didn't think about my gifts and talents and how I could use them in an emotionally satisfying way and make a living. I always thought I would have to work long hours doing something grueling to support myself. Everyone around me seemed to know what they wanted to except for me. Growing up, my mom always told me to find a need that others have and fill it with my gifts. It was not until I entered grad school and could work one-on-one with individuals in my cohort that I found my voice and understood where my strengths were. My professors often encouraged me to "speak up" because they believed I had things to say that could help others understand their strengths. I was confused. I wondered what they were talking about, but never asked them to clarify precisely what they were talking about.

Their feedback had me thinking about how I could use my insights not just to solve problems but to transform my way of seeing who I was and how I could support changes that individuals and even groups of people notice their strengths and transform the areas of their lives in which they see opportunities to gain insight and improve upon.

I never thought that what happened to me and how I handled it would illuminate what one of my messages to the world would be. Today, my favorite part of being a transformational coach is being able to facilitate healing in the lives of others. Witnessing the insights and actions of my clients is one of the most exciting and rewarding parts of using my gifts to give people opportunities to understand who they are rather than what they are doing. I believe that when I tapped into listening to others without forming assumptions about who they were, I could more readily accept that I, too, had parts of myself that weren't completely healed. Yet, I still could move forward with my aspirations and dreams without having the thought in my mind, "but I don't know enough yet," or "I'll have to think about it more."

Messages For Survivors

Certainty

I have always been a seeker. I have always wondered where everything came from and how I expected myself to function perfectly, no matter what happened to me or around me. While this may sound desirable to some, I learned to shut down my emotions when I needed to finish a workout, beat a deadline, or compete successfully. I would define overwhelm as the feeling of everything happening to me, instead of from me, all at once.

Whether there are deadlines or unexpected events, as life happens and we cannot always control what is happening or how we feel about it, I can practice accepting that what is happening is real. If I am trying to work on a project, take care of myself, and tend to the needs of others, I can accept that I feel overwhelmed.

I always ask questions about literally everything and am always looking for answers. Learning to release self-judgment, all-or-nothing thinking, shame, and denial was a challenge that took a while to overcome so that I could function and treat myself as worthy of having a chance at living.

After the incident, I lived my life in spaces where I felt like I always needed to know what was coming next. For a long time, I worked a job where I felt a sense of security in monotonous days, weeks, months, and years. These factors made me feel like I was sticking to my plan to create security and certainty in my life. I did not know it, but pursuing what I felt was security and certainty was denying the expression of my gifts and talents for the sake of what I felt was certainty.

Today, instead of looking for comfort in monotony, I have found that understanding the needs of those in my local communities and supporting people with my innate talents has proved far more fruitful than seeking certainty in every move I make.

Release Self-judgment

Today, I am far less judgmental of my emotions than I used to be. A while ago, I used to believe that uncomfortable emotions were something I should ignore or suppress with more activity. The word activity could have meant "fixing" how I felt or what was happening. Although unsure if I was toxically positive, I despised feeling "unproductive" or "stagnant." I did not realize that I could feel stagnant and unproductive, but that did not mean that I was stagnant; it just meant that I was judging myself as not being enough based on comparing myself to what others were accomplishing. With these thoughts in my mind, I could still not admit to myself that a lot of the turmoil was going on within me due to not fully accepting that I had the support I needed.

These days, I give my curious mind and my need to know, research, and understand everything during regular breaks by giving myself a chance to be in my body.

Now, this may sound strange to those who don't have a problem existing in their body, but for someone like me who used my mind to abuse my body when I did not feel like I was staying in line in the present moment and letting emotions move into my body was excruciating for me.

Today, I try to practice allowing all of me to be here without disregarding the parts of me I can barely stand. Those who have experienced bullying for their kindness, awkwardness, or any other reason should not judge themselves for having been abused and not fighting back as they believed they should. You are not responsible for the abuse you have suffered at the hands of family, acquaintances, teachers, or those you trusted to treat you with respect. The only thing that you can handle now is to stand up to the voices of abuse and to set boundaries with yourself first and others you may try to take advantage of you.

Now, I see emotions as something to be noticed rather than judged as "good" or "bad," "right" or "wrong."

Not too long ago, I believed that there must be something "wrong" within me, not knowing that if I wanted peace and freedom, I craved so much that I would have to suspend the automatic harsh judgments that I held towards myself for not responding differently in the past.

There were always voices asking myself, "Is there something wrong with me if I feel like...?" Now, I do not see any benefits in judging myself or others for how they or I should think and feel, and I now focus my mind on the things that I value rather than ruminating on who and or what I hate and what I wish would change.

This was not a onetime decision, but a decision I had to make daily. This practice has improved my relationship with myself and others in ways I had not expected. I am so much more willing to engage with people and activities that reinforce the truth of what it is to accept the gifts in my life with gratitude.

When I feel the urge to cast judgment upon myself, I ask myself, what can I create in the place of judgment that would guide me to the truth? How can I create space to receive what I need right now?

My elders always used to say to me, Statements will close minds; questions open them. Now I ask myself, "How can I open the door of my mind and heart to questions and be brave enough to find the answers?"

The Barrier of Shame

Today, I see people on the Internet on various social media platforms who create channels and forums to talk about how they feel about themselves and how society judges them for their physical attributes. Then, I'll go to the comments section and see some people encouraging them, telling them they understand how they feel and feel the same way. Other times, I see people ripping others apart for being in pain over how they're treated or how they think they are being judged. The first thought that comes to my mind is when I see people on these channels and forums sharing their experiences and how those experiences have made them feel. I'm glad that the person is talking about these experiences and how they think, but I also wonder what they are doing to heal from those experiences after bonding with people all over the world online over their wounds.

The Courage to Own My Own Truth

Although I never want to invalidate the person's feelings because acknowledging and accepting the way we feel is vital in the first steps to healing, I often wonder if they plan on taking a step to heal from these experiences other than repeatedly discussing the same things that torment them day after day.

People often accuse others of hating themselves for being judged for how they look and feel, but they are judging others for how they feel about themselves. While I believe that it's beautiful that people can acknowledge openly to the world that they are in pain, I think that sometimes, when people would rather talk about being tormented by their feelings, emotions, and thoughts and not take the next step to find healing, they are afraid of healing because they don't know who they are without their pain. I know what it is like to be so identified with developing the ability to surmount obstacles to the way I feel for not being able to take action despite the fear that I did not make room to acknowledge the feeling of weakness and then being overwhelmed by the need to hurry and heal so I can move to the next thing.

I did not want to remember the pain of being abused and mistreated. Choosing to heal meant that I had to first feel fear to feel courage. The feeling of fear can.

The same people who tell others off for feeling a certain way about how they're perceived or judged or what they look like treat themselves with the same cruelty. I know because I used to berate myself and others for having the wrong feelings about life circumstances, not completing a piece of music, getting a terrible grade, and messing up repeatedly.

However, when I stopped telling myself I was terrible at how I felt and started checking to see if I was "right" or "wrong," I could create space for the uncomfortable emotions I did not want to have.

The Courage to Own My Own Truth

The peace I experience has come from understanding that everything in life is cyclical, including emotions. There's a lot of talk in the self-help world advising people to change their thoughts about themselves and that if they change their thoughts, their lives will turn around. While I believe your thoughts play a significant role in how you see yourself in your life, I don't believe your thoughts can change without first acknowledging that your thoughts are transient daily. There's no need to force thoughts out of the mind when you decide they will come, and you, with practice, can stop assigning meanings to them that worsen your intolerance for being merely human.

For me, trying to force thoughts out of my mind and feelings out of my body by not eating destroyed me emotionally. When people try to focus all their time on being "right" or not offending someone else by telling the truth about their feelings, they abandon themselves by pretending not to have the "wrong emotions." So, authenticity is the best policy instead of trying to find the right thing to say so that nobody's offended, which isn't possible. My thoughts and feelings don't include or consider everyone on Earth, and I'm OK with that.

Healing is more of an individual decision than I had initially thought. I had to go within and decide what my personal needs and desires were and how I would create safety within myself in the future when the feelings of rage and frustration dominated my body.

Not understanding who or what I could trust after what happened to me, I had to create an atmosphere in my life where I could listen to my inner guidance without fear. This was no simple task. I kept telling myself, "Well, if I could not figure out what was at the root of my fears at that moment, then something must have been wrong with me. Developing an eating disorder after the incident and everything else around it. What the hell did I ever know?" It looked so much different from how it had been before. Today, I understand that if painful things or things I was uncomfortable with came up and I tried to silence them with distractions, it would only make the problems more extensive and overwhelming than I could have imagined. Acknowledging and accepting how I felt and thought was a whole new way of being in the world, and I would have to get into the habit of living from a place of understanding something I still have so much to learn about.

Accepting What Happened to Me

For months, I could not accept what happened to me. Since the incident, I have spoken with victims of abuse who swear they would never tell a soul what happened to them. I completely understand why because I know how it feels to expect to be judged by people who think that the victim must have experienced the abuse. Maybe the victim, like me, initially believed that the person had feelings for them, but then they discovered the person was only trying to exploit them and felt foolish for not somehow intuitively knowing that the person was a deranged pervert. Either way, something I would have offered myself in hindsight would be to treat my abuser the same way I would treat someone who jumped on me in the street in a dark alley. There is no other way to treat someone who would do such a thing. I could not let myself do that because I was too busy trying to expect the reactions I might get from other people. It took me months to decide how to handle what happened because I refused to accept it. I thought to myself: Who will believe me? Will people think I brought this on myself?

What if no one believes me? Acceptance would have meant that I felt fear and confusion and allowed myself to feel all the anxiety that comes with such a violation and speak up, anyway.

That many people know this person makes it even worse than an attack from a stranger. My inability to accept the fact that I was dealing with a dangerous monster reinforced my belief that my emotions did not matter.

It also reinforced to the abuser that he was above the law and that he could continue to abuse me, my friends, and my colleagues. That was the last thing I wanted. However, I blocked myself from this because I did not want to feel and accept how hurt and angry the incident made me think.

I advise someone who has been abused to engage in a conversation over text or e-mail and tactfully prompt the person to admit to their actions indirectly. Casually bring it up and subtly get them to admit indirectly to what they did.

Some people might say to me that this might be hard to do, but we must remember in the mind of a predator, brutalizing and abusing people is no big deal, so most of them won't have any problem admitting it to you in writing.

Third, always warn your friends and colleagues about the person who abused you so they know what could happen to them.

Be sure that you show them and police the text messages and any emails that prove what they did to you so that your friends don't become victims of their abuse. Those of us who seek to protect and care for each other need to stand up to the people who abuse us.

Stop Believing Everything That You Think

In the era we live in now, people must deal with information overload. Knowledge is no longer power. I see power is now protecting my peace as I decide what types of information can be fruitful and what types are there as distractions.

With all the information available today, many teachings and belief systems tell us we are good or bad, depending on how we feel about everything and anything. The truth is how we relate to all opinions and thoughts decides whether we can allow ourselves to create a sense of inner peace.

Even new ideologies have arisen from people's desire not to be in the bodies they were born in, which tells us we have to tell people they are the opposite of who they are for them to feel validated. What happens when people realize that the only solution to their torment is accepting that?

People want to change their outer appearance to be lighter or darker, thinner or fatter, even male or female because they feel like they do not matter as they are. We want attention and affirmation for our staying in pain because we want to avoid the challenging task of building the inner resources to accept who we are.

The Courage to Own My Own Truth

What I think people are missing here is that if you hate yourself for things that you cannot change, i.e., the body that you were born in or the mind that struggles to find peace, the body that you are disgusted by, you have no chance to heal because you are not acknowledging and accepting the things you cannot change.

While we have access to cosmetic surgeries, drugs, drinks, diets, ideologies, personas, and religions that we can hide behind, nothing can take the place of acceptance of who we are right now.

The hardest thing for people today to accept is what they think will bring them peace, whether it is their outside appearance, the emotions that torment them, or the thoughts that they hi-jack from others because they don't want to feel their feelings, will not be resolved without the daily choice to accept that the only thing they can do to heal from emotional torment is to allow themselves to feel what they feel and not be deceived into abusing themselves because of what their thoughts tell them. I say this because I abused and punished my body for the terrible feelings I felt.

Again, healing cannot occur when we chase outer appearances, whether there are physical or emotional appearances or experiences we wish to have or what we think is behind them. After chasing appearances of all kinds of things becomes dark, we realize we handle our emotional healing.

It's tough to accept that no one can or will do the transformational healing work for you, me, or anyone else. I learned to accept that no number of accomplishments I was proud of or the appearance of having myself "together" took the place of choosing to heal authentically. I also had to accept that healing is not a one-off event. It's a daily choice to decriminalize us for being humans and everything that comes with it. No individual, group of people, event, or experience can prevent me from making the daily choice to accept that I will never be close to perfect and that I do not even need to feel like I am, to seem like I am, to be loveable or loved.

The Courage to Own My Own Truth

Not so long ago, I thought that there were proper ways to feel about things and wrong ways to feel about specific thoughts, emotions, trauma, my looks, feelings, social issues, politics, and religion, not realizing that letting myself understand that there are many triggering facts around everything and any problems that people are facing.

Now, I'm learning that instead of labeling and pathologizing every emotion, thought, and circumstance I find myself in, I can give those parts a voice and let them be there without letting them consume me.

Acceptance is the most powerful practice that I have ever embraced. For so long, I had it all turned around in the opposite direction. I thought that to heal, I needed to fix myself and then try to learn to accept my new fixed self when I needed to learn to admit that I was how I am where I am and that I could make the inner changes that I needed to make with support from people who love me as I am and see the potential in me to cultivate the discipline, courage, and resilience to develop trust within myself.

Accepting support from other people who had been through the same things that I had been through or even just people that could help me always made me uneasy because I was always wondering when they were going to find out how screwed up I was and leave me to rot. That was just another lie I told myself because I did not want to accept that there were people who loved me enough to tell me the truth and stay by my side, whether I seemed perfect or "good enough" in my own eyes.

The Importance of Owning Your Narrative

After someone violated me, I swore I would tell no one. It was my story; in my eyes, it was buried. What I didn't realize is that by not telling my story, I wasn't just burying the incident of what happened to me; I was burying parts of myself that I did not want ever to surface. I thought that staying silent would protect me from criticism and any chance of not being believed. The fact that what had happened was so common that it even occurred to me was beyond my comprehension. Like many people, I could not accept that this was a life-changing event.

Before, I had so many thoughts, primarily concerning what others would think rather than how I would cope emotionally. I was so used to being fine and shutting off the parts of me I didn't want to deal with that I had become an expert at denying anything that brought me discomfort around who I was. I used to believe that denial was something that protected me and kept me safe from having to wrestle with the pain and disappointment that life sometimes brought to me, thinking that if things went wrong, then I must have done something wrong, or I needed to man up and move on like the strong black woman that I am. I'll save that topic for another book if there is just too much to unpack in that statement.

When I talk about owning your own story, I mean getting it down on paper with a pen and only stopping writing once you understand you are a human being worthy of compassion and understanding for how you responded. Acknowledge yourself as a person who can completely heal if you choose what happened to you.

Maybe you don't want to tell your story now. Still, suppose you decide to tell your story. In that case, the benefits will outweigh the consequences because at least you can move on to the following chapters of your life, knowing that you are not responsible for that person who abused you. And that you can help other people open up about how they treat themselves when they're broken and in pain.

To this day, I have still not told my parents that I developed an eating disorder after an incident of sexual abuse because I still feel like I don't want to burden them with all of me. I still have work to do in my relationships with my family, and I fully accept that it may never change.

Owning my story is an ongoing evolution of accepting all of my parts, even those I have been ashamed of for so long. But I wrote this book because I no longer maintain the self-hatred of being a person who has needs, wants, and desires. There are things in my life that I can control, and there are things I cannot. What I can control is how I decide to relate to my pain and how I decide to use my strength and resilience to foster healing in my life.

The Courage to Own My Own Truth

I found the shame and the judgment that I thought the people I love would have of me were all in my head.

Now I understand if people love and care about me, they'll listen to my story and maybe believe me; if they don't, that's not my responsibility to make them. My responsibility is to empower people, give them the hope they need to accept what happened, and accept that healing is a right that you can exercise if you have any hope of living with yourself authentically.

Your story is essential. It is your story to tell and no one else's. When you own your own story, you can open the door to healing your emotions and regaining trust in yourself to stand up for yourself and other victims of abuse and live without shame, free from the confines of the lies of self-hatred.

About the Author

Elisabeth Henderson is an author based in Dallas, Texas, who is passionate about empowering people's voices and ensuring they are heard. Henderson's writing is dedicated to shedding light on unheard stories and her own experiences with anxiety disorders, PTSD, OCD, and eating disorders.

When she's not immersed in her writing, Henderson finds solace and inspiration in her hobbies. Her love for music, expressed through her harp playing, and her passion for movement, evident in her social dancing and roller-skating, are integral parts of her life. These activities not only enrich her life but also fuel her creativity as a writer, allowing her to draw inspiration from different art forms.

Henderson's dedication to amplifying marginalized voices and addressing crucial issues is not confined to her writing. She is a true advocate for change, actively participating in philanthropic efforts.

Her Master's degree in Business Leadership and Management, coupled with her experience as a volunteer, coach, and consultant, equips her with the tools to empower individuals to find their voices.

She leads by example in both professional and charitable endeavors. She is also a frustrated sight-reader and proud cat mother who has visited 25 states and enjoys traveling internationally.

The Courage to Own My Own Truth

From the Publisher

Dear Reader,

If you've reached this page, you've journeyed through a story of resilience, strength, and the power of speaking out. You've read a tale of survival; perhaps it resonated with your own.

I am Jean Dorff, author of Broken Silence and founder of The Empowering Story Program. I understand the courage it takes to share your story, for I have walked that path. I also know the healing and liberation of owning and sharing your narrative with the world.

The Empowering Story Program helps survivors of sexual abuse do just that. We believe in the power of storytelling as a tool for healing, empowerment, and inspiring others. Our motto is: 'I Tell My Story, so there is One Less Story to Tell.'

We are here to guide you through transforming your story into a published book. In 90 days or less, guaranteed, your story can be in the hands of those who need to hear it most.

The Courage to Own My Own Truth

Sharing your story is not just about you. It's about the countless others who, like you, have experienced abuse.

Your story can inspire them to break their silence, seek help, and begin their healing journey.

If you're ready to own your story of sexual abuse and publish it as a book, we're here to help.

Follow this link
https://theempoweringstory.com to start your journey towards healing, empowerment, and inspiring others.

Remember, your voice matters. Your story matters. Together, we can reduce the number of untold stories.

With hope and courage,

Jean Dorff Founder and Owner

The Empowering Story
https://theempoweringstory.com

Made in the USA
Columbia, SC
08 September 2024

41969079R00085